DEMOCRACY, EAST AND WEST

Democracy finds itself in rather quizzical circumstances in our time. In the United Nations, anti-Western blocks of nations are using venerable Western parliamentary institutions to subvert the perceived interests of Western democracies. In the military sphere, on the other hand, these Western democracies, perceiving communism as a mortal enemy, are propping up brutal or corrupt dictators who happen to be anti-communist, or supporting the subversion of Marxist governments which happen to be supported by the majority of their citizenry. But then again, many Marxist governments, aiming for the democratic–egalitarian ideal of a classless society and control by workers of their own lives, find themselves perpetuating new species of class privileges and quashing legitimate workers' movements.

Obviously democracy, which during the eighteenth-century Enlightenment seemed to offer a much-desired escape from arbitrary class structures and oppressive governments, has not proven to be a sure formula or simple solution. An awareness of the true complexities of democracy requires an understanding of a perennial dialectic residing at the heart of democracy, and manifesting itself in specific dialectical relationships: between élitism and populism, liberty and equality, smallness and bigness, religion and secular life, politics and economics, etc. Such dialectical relationships, originally most explicit in particular nations, are now becoming unmistakably manifest in international relations.

An awareness of this larger dialectic, in which the "Western", "communist", and "third-world" blocs are all unavoidably involved at present, supplies an important prerequisite for the consideration of specific ideological problems arising out of current impasses. For example, should the Western democracies disband the current United Nations organization and reestablish an organization whose membership would be limited to liberal democracies? Since nuclear annihilation threatens the continued existence of all nations, is it not imperative to accept any plan with high probability for halting the arms race, even if this requires "non-democratic" measures? And in view of all the problems apparently endemic in democracy, is it still justified to subscribe to democracy as "the last best hope" of mankind.

Dr. Howard P. Kainz is a Professor of Philosophy at Marquette University, Milwaukee, Wisconsin, and specializes in German philosophy, political philosophy and philosophical anthropology. His previous books are *Hegel's Philosophy of Right, with Marx's Commentary*, *The Unbinding of Prometheus*, *Ethica Dialectica*, *The Philosophy of Man* and *Hegel's Phenomenology Parts I and II*. He was a National Endowment for the Humanities Fellow in 1977–78 and a Fulbright fellow in Germany in 1981–82.

DEMOCRACY EAST AND WEST
A Philosophical Overview

Howard P. Kainz

AN AUTHORS GUILD BACKINPRINT.COM
EDITION

iUNIVERSE, INC.
BLOOMINGTON

Democracy East & West
A Philosophical Overview

iUniverse books may be ordered through booksellers or by contacting:

iUniverse
1663 Liberty Drive
Bloomington, IN 47403
www.iuniverse.com
1-800-Authors (1-800-288-4677)

ISBN: 978-1-4502-7640-5 (sc)

Printed in the United States of America

iUniverse rev. date: 3/18/2011

Contents

Acknowledgements

A Marquette University Summer Faculty Fellowship in 1974 gave me the opportunity for initial research on this book. I received some very useful critiques of earlier versions of the book from my colleagues in philosophy, Bill Starr and the late Thomas Davitt, S. J. The final version was read and critiqued by Wayne Wheeler of the Department of Political Science at Marquette and by Jim Dougherty of the Department of Politics at St Joseph's College in Philadelphia, indexed by A. J. Thomas of Des Plaines, Illinois, and proofread by Brad Wronsky, a Marquette University graduate fellow. For the imperfections still remaining after all this much-appreciated expert assistance, I assume full responsibility.

Introduction: Democracy and Political Philosophy

The purpose of this book is to re-examine some of the pivotal concepts considered essential to, or frequently associated with, democracy, and the way in which these concepts are applied in contemporary political systems. However, when we consider the various contenders in the worldwide pursuit of democratic orthodoxy, it becomes immediately obvious that the term, 'democracy', is being used to describe almost every species of political system now prevalent except for an out-and-out non-socialist dictatorship. Thus we must be aware at the outset of the danger of developing a definition of democracy so diluted that it becomes meaningless.

American democracy, one of the largest and most committed democratic systems, can at least offer us a convenient starting point (if not the paradigm that it claims to offer) for our consideration of modern, 'Western', *liberal* democracy. The latter political form is sometimes described, and possibly idealised, as a form of government which prides itself on its recognition of, and commitment to, individual freedoms and personal property rights. Whether or not in practice it really champions these values, at least in such a way as not to compromise other values and principles to which it is equally committed, is another question – which we will also take up. But we must not ignore the fact that there are other paradigms, besides what Americans might call 'liberal' democracies, and many other claimants to the title of 'democratic'. And so, while returning frequently to the situations and problematics in the American model, I will also consider European, Israeli, and Marxist versions of democracy, and even investigate whether (*per impossible*) they might possibly have certain things in common.

But to compare the American model of democracy with other models will be a formidable undertaking, should we wish to bring in to the reckoning certain commonly held American ideological 'givens'. For among political scientists nowadays, it is generally accepted that

American 'political philosophy' is almost an 'extinct species' in our intellectual milieu, although we sometimes try to delude ourselves that we have a viable political philosophy. For example, Daniel Boorstin observes that 'no nation has ever believed more firmly than America that its political life was based on a perfect theory . . . and yet no nation has ever been less interested in political philosophy or produced less in the way of theory'.[1] Boorstin believes there would be a fundamental inconsistency in our asking any other country to adopt our philosophy of government because purely and simply we 'have no philosophy which can be exported'. Robert Dahl, whose *Preface to Democratic Theory* has had an important impact on political thought in the last couple of decades, concurs in Boorstin's indictment: 'There is no democratic theory,' Dahl tells us, 'only democratic theories',[2] a pluralistic mass of conflicting ideological claims or nostrums, none of which can be taken to portray democracy absolutely. Neal Riemer in *A Revival of Democratic Theory* includes an extensive survey of current consensus in political science – the opinions of thinkers such as Hans Morganthau and Leo Strauss – to the effect that what is called 'political theory' in the democratic tradition now simply amounts to an account of past thought ('classical' political theories) and has altogether abandoned what used to be considered the central question in political philosophy: 'what is the best political order?'[3] He traces this unconcern for theory to the negative overreaction in the democratic 'West' to the exaggerated emphasis on highly systematised theories found in totalitarian political systems. Arnold Brecht sees this generally antagonistic attitude towards political theory as particularly a twentieth-century development, and ascribes the trend to the general upsurge in the use and prestige of the supposedly axiologically neutral and philosophically 'unprejudiced' 'scientific method' in all areas of thought.[4] The political scientist is supposed, namely, to focus on the actually given facts and quantities in the political sphere, and eschew 'theory-making' in the old-fashioned, classical sense.

Lest we take these samples as indications of a concerted agreement about the demise of political philosophy proper, however, we must advert to a definite equivocity from all quarters regarding the *precise* meaning of 'political philosophy'. For some, the terms 'political philosophy' and 'political theory' seem to be rather synonymous, while others describe a 'political theorist' as a kind of high-level tactician who mediates between the strict empiricist and the linguistic 'political philosopher', the latter being one who applies 'linguistic analysis' to political matters.[5] Others see political philosophy as the 'normative' sub-division of the more all-encompassing 'political theory', which is supposed to integrate empirical, normative *and* prudential aspects (the 'is', the 'ought' and the 'science of the possible').[6] Many analytic philosophers understandably enough tend to reserve the term 'political philosophy' for what they themselves are doing – namely, subjecting political needs and principles to a straightforward conceptual and/or linguistic analysis.[7] Some analysts, however, such as Rawls and Nozick, have made noteworthy attempts to rise above these conventional restrictions, often by a reversion to Kantian norms of moral rationality.

If we were to concentrate just on the latter, and on political thinkers outside the analytical tradition, and search for a consensus concerning the meaning of 'political philosophy', without making any mention of the term, 'political theory' – we would probably come up with a 'majority opinion' to the effect that political philosophy is legitimately concerned with the non-empirical, 'normative' aspects of the political sphere – the 'ought', including moralistic and utopian as well as all value-oriented political thinking.

It is customary, among those who strive to define more precisely what is meant by political philosophy as a normative or 'prescriptive' approach to the study of politics, to contrast this approach with the strictly empirical or 'descriptive' observation and analysis of political structures and activities characterizing 'political science' proper. There is, however, a goodly portion of the weeds of contemporary myth growing up alongside of the sapling 'reality' of political science, and it is necessary to distinguish these weeds from the real thing, with a view to separating the two, once that recognition is accomplished.

In sociology and psychology, as well as in political studies, it has long been thought that the use of strictly scientific procedures after the pattern of the physical sciences would provide the key to unlimited human progress. In the eighteenth century, pathfinders such as Beccaria and Condorcet tried to develop a mathematically precise and empirically based science of human organisation and progress, modeled after Newton's approach to physics.[8] In the nineteenth century, August Comte, Vilfredo Pareto and others, using a more Baconian model, inaugurated a social science which distanced itself abruptly from classical political philosophy by insisting on the use of the methods which were standard in the physical sciences – observation, experimentation, and systematic logical induction from facts. At the turn of the century there were attempts to counterbalance static descriptive studies of institutions with a Darwinian perceptiveness concerning factual (social) development, and in the last few decades political scientists, following the lead of stimulus–response studies in behavioural psychology, have concentrated on the effects of 'input' from the social environment on the 'output' of the political system or systems proper.[9] In all of these laudable attempts to render the study of human society more scientific, the myth has been that exact scientific procedures could be used to gather and evaluate human and social facts and to arrive via the route of inductive generalisations at incontrovertible conclusions accepted universally within the 'scientific community' (the term being applied here to researchers specifically in the social sciences). The reality always turns out to be that the social sciences are immeasurably more complex than the physical and even the biological sciences. In the sphere of human behaviour and interaction, it is difficult to get any agreement as to just what the unadulterated 'facts' are, let alone arrive at any inductive generalisations from these facts. And even if we do locate some relatively incontrovertible facts to be fed into our calculating brains and computers, the inductive generalisations we arrive at have even less validity than the so-called 'laws of nature' which are the products of induction in physics, and which thinkers as far apart intellectually as Hegel and Hans Reichenbach have shown to be at best educated guesses and mere probabilities.[10] Some researchers in the 'soft' sciences, chiefly psychologists, have demonstrated some of the almost insurmountable obstacles in avoiding value-laden presuppositions in carrying out some ostensibly objective research projects: the 'facts' that we choose, and the kinds of questions we ask about them, betray all kinds of emotional, unscientific bias.[11] And all in all, it is ironic that the social sciences are still trying to imitate the idealised objectivity of physics, at a time when physicists and other 'hard' scientists – under the impetus of Heisenberg's Indeterminacy Principle and other twentieth-century developments – have given up the pursuit of pure objectivity!

But in the camp of the 'other side' – the political philosophers – perfectly pure hands are just as rare a find. Political philosophers such as Hobbes and Hegel have been criticised (sometimes justly) for spinning speculative webs of what seem to be insightful values or 'oughts' but which at base are nothing but subtle and often elaborate justifications of the status quo ('the present form of government is *necessary* because of such-and-such abstract principles, and therefore ought to remain in *perpetuum*'); others, such as Plato and Marx have been criticised (sometimes justly) for the opposite reason – propounding 'scientific' utopian ideas which are simply conceptual elaborations of their own emotional *resentment* towards the existing political regime, and thus are pseudo-'oughts', norms which as negative reactions are so out of touch with empirical realities that they are not really viable and relevant norms at all. In between these two extremes we have a few political philosophers – Aristotle and Locke and Kant might be included in this group – who by avoiding Scylla and Charibdis have entitled themselves to a healthy respect and a greater acceptance in the West.

There is, however, some disagreement as to whether political philosophy of *any* stripe or species would be relevant and useful to a *democracy*. We spoke above of a *factual* disinterest in political philosophy or ideology. There seems to be a growing consensus, and some elaborate theorising, to the effect that this factual disinterest is a necessity and even a virtue in democracy. For example, according to Frankel, there seems to be a basic contradiction in the very idea of a political philosophy (understood as an ideology made explicit and exoteric) in the context of a democracy which, to his mind, implies almost 'by definition' the freedom of everyone to pursue his or her own *individual* ideal or ideals.[12] 'Heaven' (including those political philosophers who have well-worked-out ideals and ultimates) he tells us, 'has no need of a democracy.' It is precisely bungling and fallible [and presumably a- or anti-philosophical] beings like the 'practical Americans' who need democracy. Democracy is *ex professo* a type of government which eschews ideology and ultimate principles.[13] (Presumably a nation of idealistic normative philosophers would be inherently incompetent to settle upon democratic norms.) Boorstin is of the same sentiment, telling us that the lack of political philosophy is one of the keys to the 'genius' of the American people: since Americans do not try to break up their life into unwieldly dichotomies between 'ought' and 'is', etc., the salutary result is a kind of 'seamlessness' and ineluctable coherence in their given experience.[14] R. Wollheim, perhaps trying to make a virtue out of what he deems to be a necessity, hypothesises that since it is impossible for anyone to know what is right for the whole community, everyone should be allowed to do what he wants to do as far as socially possible, living uninhibited by definite ideology, and habituated to ingrained scepticism, such as is possible preeminently in democracy.[15] P. H. Partridge, in a more conciliatory frame of mind, simply observes that in actual practice the broad consensus found in democracy may have taken the place of the ideological structures which used to be necessary (as underpinnings or superstructures) to assure the success of political systems in the days of yore.[16] David Ingersoll, finally, in *Communism, Fascism and Democracy* contrasts democracy with other systems specifically on the basis of its complete neutrality as far as philosophy is concerned – democracy is a unique form of government in which *any* kind of philosophy, idealistic, dualistic or materialistic, can coexist peacefully with the realities of political praxis.[17]

It should not escape our notice that all the above-mentioned authors, in disclaiming the importance of ideology or philosophy[18] to democracy, are, in the very positions they are taking, expounding an ideology, albeit an ideology of relativism or scepticism. Would not it be preferable to point out in a more positive vein that an ideology in a 'liberal' democracy is going to have to differ considerably from some of the other overly rigid and repressive ideologies with which we are familiar, and then proceed to try to develop our own 'liberal' democratic ideology in a positive and constructive manner?

However, the negative attitude towards ideology in a democracy *has* elicited some countercurrents: Sanford Lakoff, after a long and detailed analysis of the idea of 'equality' in a democracy, remarks that 'the conclusion seem inescapable that whether or not we believe in the ultimate ability of social science to clear up all difficulties in the realm of value, and whether or not we accept the contentions of analytic philosophy that clarification of words and ideas is the necessary and sufficient task of contemporary philosophy, we remain in need . . . of something very much like political philosophy, i.e. an attempt outside the analytic tradition, to re-examine values and even prescribe values'.[19] Brecht laments the proven impotence of democratic 'political science' in its encounter with the formidable and devastatingly dangerous ideologies of Fascism and Naziism during World War II.[20] Riemer warns that the lack of explicit theory in Western democracy can be as dangerous as that ideology *ad nauseam* which has characterised both communism and fascism. And Walter Burnham in a recent article sounds the clarion call for a 'new American ideology' which will serve to bring about that minimal centralisation which is necessary for reconciling all the competing interest groups in contemporary America.[21]

'Ideology', as we have seen, can be used in a pejorative or in a positive sense. In the positive sense, it does not always denote strictly philosophical theories (having direct or indirect political applications). It may also refer to a political ideology such as whig theory, which happened also to be developed and justified by philosophers such as

John Locke. In either positive use of the term, it would be misleading to say outright that America is lacking an ideology. The explicit and stable underpinning of American political thought through Whig ideology has been sufficiently and ably argued by Donald Lutz, Gordon Wood and others. Less widely recognised is the ideological centrality in America of the philosophy of pragmatism, as expounded by Peirce, James, Dewey, Mead and others. If there is a sense in which an elaborate philosophical system (here 'systematic method' would be a more appropriate term than 'system') develops out of the special genius of a nation, makes explicit its values and *modus operandi*, and distills the essence of some of its basic principles by a process of meta-empirical generalisation – pragmatism is the 'official' philosophy of America, at least the only original philosophy it has ever produced.[22] Quite a few authors have observed that pragmatism, which purports to discern and/or clarify meanings and/or values on the basis of actual and/or possible effects, seems to sum up quite well the inherently practical experimental, wait-and-see attitude of a nation which is devoted to science, invention, technology and a healthy relativism which facilitates social and political progress. However there has been no noticeable concerted effort among 'card-carrying' pragmatists to make explicit application of their philosophical method to the realm of political philosophy. Perhaps the closest approximation to this is to be found in Dewey's *Ethics* (1908), *Democracy and Education* (1916), *Liberalism and Social Action* (1935), and *Freedom and Culture* (1939), all of which try to show in a somewhat popularised fashion, the relevance of the progressive = experimental = 'instrumental' = 'pragmatic' approach to the furtherance of the American way of life and democratic institutions.

But at any rate attempts to apply official and highly structured philosophical systems/constructs/principles/methods to the 'practical realm' (including politics, ethics and the arts) have never been notable for their spectacular success and permanent impress in the evolution of cultures. In 'applied ethics' it would be hard to find one clear-cut and eminently persuasive instance of the Kantian categorical imperative, or the scholastic–Thomistic principle of 'double effect', or the utilitarians' principle of 'the greatest happiness for the greatest number' or Dewey's pragmatic 'rule of thumb' that the value of something is proportionate to, and only relevant to, the beneficial results it will imply or entail for those who possess it, make use of it, etc. Probably the two most noteworthy attempts to apply definite and elaborate principles in political philosophy or practical politics have been the Leninist version of Marxism and the Nazi potpourri (concocted by Alfred Rosenberg and other 'official' Nazi 'philosophers') of *a priori* Hegelian, Wagnerian, and Nietzschean principles to political propaganda and planning – and neither of these attempts is noted for clearly and unequivocally elevating the level of political life and discourse.

The implications must be faced squarely: if the relevance and importance of political philosophy hinges on the ability of semi-official political philosophies (and philosophers) to supply definite and clearly-worked-out guidelines for political activity and thinking, the 'sceptics' alluded to above are probably correct: democracy probably can function well, even optimally, unhampered by such ideological superstructures. Even such hallowed 'Lockean' principles as liberty and 'majority rule' in the American democratic system can be counterproductive and even dangerous to democratic institutions if applied in a wholesale, strict, and literal way, as we shall show in some of the chapters which follow.

But political philosophy does not necessarily have to mean a definite set of abstractions or principles elaborated into an intellectual system or methodology. Creative and progressive moral philosophising has been taking place throughout history (sometimes by professional philosophers, most often by those who would not be designated specifically as philosophers) under impetus of impelling, challenging and inescapable moral problems or dilemmas. Creative political and social philosophising has been taking place with similar regularity under similar conditions by thinkers under many auspices (some philosophers, some psychologists, no doubt many 'political scientists', and others).

As we align, or try to align ourselves with this group, however, one thing becomes clear: the sharp divisions which are often made, 'descriptive' vs. 'prescriptive', 'empirical' vs. 'normative', are artificial and unwarranted. In particular, the stereotype of a purely normative kind of political philosophising which 'transcends experience', must be discarded, as well as the stereotype of the strictly and conscientiously 'descriptive' political scientist. The boundaries are not, and never have been, that clear-cut.

(1) The empirical analysis of 'states of affairs' and 'what is going on' can and must be extended as follows: The 'facts' that political science must deal with are not only the first-order phenomena but also second-order 'phenomena' such as the very *relationship* between facts and values; and it is not only peripheral movements of the machinery

of government and political parties and pressure groups and the 'people' that is 'going on', but also the conflict of ideologies (which are often *a priori* presuppositions about the nature of man or the nature of communities), and the explicit or implicit prescription of norms for action by various individuals and likewise the conflicts between these norms and the inevitable choices that must be made among them, by individuals as well as societies. And the process of 'observation' in scientific method can be extended, without necessarily any contradiction or any impropriety, to *introspective* phenomena, personal and subjective facts which make up (in importance and significance) for what they lack in public accessibility and 'consubjectivity.'[23] And finally, the process of scientific *experimentation* can be extended to the 'weighing' and 'measuring' of, and impact and resistance tests on, values; Brecht, for example, suggests that studies in comparative government could be something like 'laboratory tests' in the realm of political science.[24]

(2) Likewise, conceptual analysis and deductive thinking – after the pattern of Aristotle's analysis of justice, Hobbes' analysis of authority, Locke's and Rousseau's theorising about the origins of political community – will do best to avoid an empirical vacuum. It would be absurd, for example, to analyse the state in terms of some sort of original 'social contract' if those who make up the state at present *do not think of their own state* as being constituted originally, or about to be reconstituted in the near future, in this way. Thus 'social contract' theories are likely to be more relevant and applicable to societies which are threatened by usurpation of authority or are encountering the possibility or actuality of reconstitution through revolution or civil upheaval. (Whether or not there actually, factually was, in some primitive era, something amounting to a 'social contract' is a matter of interest to anthropology, not to political philosophy. Even if an élite corps of anthropologists proved such an initial contract, and yet the vast cross-section of people *in a state* could not assent to the proof which the anthropologists offered, it would be quixotic to philosophise on the basis of any such theory with reference to *that particular state*.) Again, it would be ludicrous for a philosopher to expound on some natural law for which there was not a broad consensus of the citizenry (as an extreme example: speaking about a natural law forbidding cannibalism to a society in which all members practised, or at least believed in, cannibalism). And certainly a great part of what a philosopher does, if he is going to be accepted and even *understood*, will involve merely making explicit, or bringing to the surface,

attitudes which have been latent in the notions of 'givenness' already subscribed to by the people he is addressing – an 'empirical' undertaking, to a great extent. Boorstin in *The Genius of American Politics*[25] points to the process of such explication as an 'alternative' to political philosophy; but G. W. F. Hegel, who was irrefutably a political philosopher in some sense of the word, describes his own procedure in philosophising in similar terms – i.e. as making explicit the second-order empirical 'givens' (ideas and values) which have already matured in the body politic and are ready for the 'picking'.[26]

Both Boorstin and Hegel emphasise that the discernment of *potentialities* in social and political interactions is a worthy object of attention. And in taking this position, they are echoing the words with which Rousseau begins his *Social Contract*: '[The purpose of political philosophy] is to consider if, in political society, there can be any legitimate and sure principle of government, taking men as they *are* and laws as they *can* [peuvent] be.' (Italics added.)

It is this double focus on the actual and the possible, and the complementary interest in an 'ought' based on the 'can', which I would like to contribute to, and perpetuate, in this book.

NOTES

1. *The Genius of American Politics* (University of Chicago Press, 1953) p. 8.
2. Op. cit. (University of Chicago Press, 1965) p. 1.
3. Op. cit. (NY: Appleton-Century Crofts, 1962) ch. 1.
4. *Political Theory: the Foundations of Twentieth Century Political Thought* (Princeton University Press, 1959). The 'death' of political philosophy was solemnly announced to the English-speaking world by Peter Laslett in the Introduction to *Philosophy, Politics and Society* (Oxford: Basil Blackwell, 1956). Numerous other works in the 1950s and early 1960s concluded the *post mortems*.
5. See John Plamenatz' article, 'The Uses of Political Theory' in A. Quinton's *Political Philosophy* (Oxford University Press, 1967).
6. See Reimer, op. cit., Introduction.
7. Even within this tradition there is some ambiguity, however, as to just what the proximate subject-matter for conceptual analysis should be: Should it be concerned with methodological and structural problems developing specifically out of political science proper? Or should it deal with political opinions, principles and values actually prevalent in the 'body politic?'
8. For an especially thorough treatment of these developments, see Garry Wills, *The Inventing of America* (NY: Doubleday, 1978) pp. 95, 140ff, 150ff.

9. For an extensive discussion of methodology in modern political science, see *The Limits of Behaviorism in Political Science* J. Charlesworth, ed. (Philadelphia: American Academy of Political and Social Science, 1962).
10. Arnold Brecht, op. cit., I, 2 analyses the historical progress of the critical analysis of scientific method and induction, and shows the relevance of the criticisms in particular to political science.
11. Although it may be possible to avoid bringing one's values consciously into the process of scientific inquiry, nevertheless in social science a special type of knowledge is valued and the investigator's values certainly enter into his choice of a topic and the object of study is often this or that individual or public value which may or may not jibe with the chief investigator's personal values.
12. *The Democratic Prospect* (NY: Harper, 1962) p. 171.
13. Ibid., p. 27.
14. The *Genius of American Politics*, p. 175.
15. 'Democracy', *Journal of the History of Ideas*, XIX, 1958.
16. 'Politics, Philosophy, Ideology', in *Political Philosophy*, A. Quinton, ed. (NY: Oxford University Press, 1967) p. 37.
17. Op. cit. (Ohio: Merrill Publishing Co., 1971).
18. The political thinkers we have just mentioned tend to equate ideology with 'philosophical speculation', while a political philosopher like Maurice Cranston equates ideology with propagandistic dogma, and defines it as 'a system of thought which, in Marx's words, seeks to change the world rather than to understand it' (see 'Political Philosophy in Our Time', in *The Great Ideas Today*, Hutchins and Adler, eds, Chicago: Encyclopedia Brittanica, 1975). Thus they not only define 'ideology' in opposite ways, but are both against it for completely opposite reasons.
19. Lakoff, *Equality in Political Philosophy* (Mass : Harvard University Press, 1964) p. 237.
20. *Political Theory*, Introduction.
21. See 'Thoughts on the "Governability Crisis" in the West' in *The Washington Review of Strategic and International Studies* (July 1978).
22. Charles Morris in *The Pragmatic Movement in American Philosophy* (NY: Braziller, 1970, p. 5) points to unquestioning acceptance of American democratic ideals as a quasi-axiom of pragmatic philosophy. In a similar fashion, the group of philosophies labelled 'British empiricism' may be taken to represent values and principles, often conflicting values and principles, prevailing in the British nation, and the group of philosophies designated as German idealism may be taken to represent a world view predominant at least at the time the respective philosophies were published. We focus on pragmatism here, but similar observations might be made and have been made (see John Plamenatz, 'Some American Images of Democracy', in *The Great Ideas Today* (Chicago: Encyclopedia Brittanica, 1968) about utilitarianism, an ethical theory thriving in America and similar in thrust to pragmatism, but imported from European philosophical sources. For a contrast-comparison of pragmatism and utilitarianism, see H. Kainz, *Ethica Dialectica* (The Hague: Nijhoff, 1979) pp. 140ff.
23. Brecht, op. cit., I, 1. See also *The Limits of Behaviorism*, pp. 2f.

24. Ibid., I, 2.
25. Boorstin, op. cit., pp. 160–70.
26. See the *Philosophy of Right* (Knox, tr., NY: Oxford University Press, 1967, p. 13). It is this process of explicating latent attitudes and ideals that exonerates Hegel from the charge of *merely* defending the status quo.

1 Towards a Definition of Democracy

> In the primitive family one essential feature of civilization is still lacking. The arbitrary will of its head, the father, was unrestricted. . . . The way led from this family to the succeeding stage of communal life in the form of bands of brothers. In overpowering their father, the sons had made the discovery that a combination can be stronger than a single individual. . . . The taboo-observances were the first 'right' or 'law'. . . . One might expect that the further development of civilization would proceed smoothly towards . . . a further extension of the number of people included in the community.
>
> Freud, *Civilization and Its Discontents*

This description by Freud of the 'primal scene' and the 'primal crime' was not meant to be a metapsychological account for the development of democracy. But it does indicate that in the evolution of civilisation there has been a gradual and seminal but quite constant drift towards the appropriation of power by masses who were formerly subject to arbitrary rule of some sort.

In Aristotle's *Ethics* a similar theme is developed. There are, according to Aristotle, familial analogies in government: monarchy is an extension of fatherly or patriarchal authority: aristocracy is an extension of something like the combined rule of husband and wife; democracy reflects somewhat the comradery of brothers.

Neither Aristotle nor Freud intended to give a scientific, precise account of the anthropological origins of democracies, but they do give us some clues as to some of the basic distinguishing characteristics or 'clustering of traits' that we might look for in a democracy: wider sharing of authority, equality, fraternity, freedom, decentralisation etc.

Almost all of the reputed 'democratic' traits, however, are subject to qualification and exception: Democracies are frequently or even generally created by a violent or nonviolent revolution or rebellion, but there are instances of monarchs or patriarchal rulers voluntarily abdicating their autocratic positions to create a democracy. Democracies are noted for equality and 'fraternity'. But the spirit of fraternity is frequently marred by discords and factions (brothers never have been famous for getting along with one another); and by 'equality' we conventionally mean a spirit of toleration and fair play enforced primarily by those who are considered *equally important* in a community or state (the number of whom frequently falls far short of 100 per cent). Certainly freedom from arbitrary authority or despotism is an important motivation in the formation and preservation of democracies; however, largely legal persuasion and propaganda can sometimes generate tyrannies, as we learned from the regime of Hitler which was approved by a national plebiscite in Germany in the 1930s. The notion of self-rule ('government of the people, by the people . . .') is taken to be very important to a democracy, but it is hard to understand how the ever-present apathetic segments of citizens in a democracy who do not vote or otherwise participate in government on any level can be said to be 'ruling' themselves in any meaningful sense (although we may grant that in some cases they may be allowed by others to 'do as they please'). Some political theorists point to the 'element of disorder',[1] considered to be a sort of unspoken commitment to the principle that not too much of the life of the citizens in a democracy will be subject to control and organisation – as a characteristic of democracies; but uniformity, conformity and/or total mobilisation of a democratic people can be achieved on occasion by persuasion or subtle social pressure in lieu of any visible centralised controlling authority. There is *hardly any characteristic of democracy which proponents of Western democracy would not feel obliged to qualify*, or make exceptions to in some fashion.

Because of all of the qualifications required in ascribing such traits to democracies, one would not expect to find any one democracy which possessed all the traits. And yet if all or most of the above traits were *lacking* in a particular government, it would hardly be appropriate to refer to that government as a democracy.

Equality, liberty, self-determination, political and social pluralism – all bona fide democracies seem to be variations on these essential themes. But many accidental 'differentiating characteristics' found in the variants or mutations not only serve to individuate the several styles of democracy, but are sometimes confused with the more essential traits, and thus taken to be *sine qua nons* for *all* democracies.

In the ancient Greek variant, the following individuating characteristics are often referred to: (a) *The idea that democracy was the 'rule of the poor'*[2] (the Greek term, *demos*, connoted the unpropertied masses). This idea has a semblance of truth insofar as in any transition from a more aristocratic form of government to a government with more widely shared 'self-rule', those to whom the self-rule is being newly extended will, relatively speaking, be less 'propertied' than the average person or persons who possessed political power previously. But although democracy has frequently fallen under the control of the poorer classes,[3] the ascendency has been achieved by what we might call the 'middle-class' when the latter class found itself to constitute an effective majority. (b) *The notion of 'full participation'* as an important or even *the* most important characteristic of a democracy. In the Greek (Athenian) variant, this popular political participation was manifested by the ideally plenary (but in actuality less-than-plenary) sessions of the assemblies of the citizens, which often made direct decisions by vote on laws, policies and other important matters. This model is considered inimitable in most modern democratic states, which are too large and unwieldy to make laws and decisions in popular assemblies, and whose citizens, in spite of rapid transportation, industrialisation and automation, do not have the leisure afforded to many citizens of the Athenian city-state by the almost universal practice of slavery flourishing there and then. (c) *The practice of choosing many leaders by lot*. This method was no doubt preferable to the imposition of leadership by a hostile 'tyrant', and was facilitated by the fact that the minority who were actually counted as bona fide 'citizens' were roughly equal and, to a certain extent, interchangeable. Selection by lot is certainly no worse than the rather haphazard and uninformed manner in which present-day citizens of democracies make many of their choices at the polls. But it is certainly unconscionable in a social milieu characterised by great diversification (if not downright 'inequality'). (d) *The final review* at the end of the term of public office for certain officials, a routine process which could result in drastic consequences, even death sentences. Such a process could help keep elected officials honest, but could also have the effect of making them overly obsequious to the known values or whims of the judging body, to which they were answerable. As democratic wisdom has evolved and matured, we have come to realise that such a practice could have a deleterious effect at least on the objectivity and responsibility of certain officials – e.g. judges – who *ex officio* are often called on to exercise independent judgement and resist influential nostrums.[4]

Finally, (e) *the notion that democracy was feasible only in a relatively small and homogeneous society*. The ancients could not even visualise a large grouping of cities, towns and villages in which the interaction and intercommunication requisite for a democracy would prevail.[5]

In the last three centuries, new variants of democracy have arisen which, in addition to some of what we have called the 'essential' traits, boasted features which are scarcely found in any of the ancient models.[6] Some of these special traits are: (a) a particular concern for validating and perpetuating certain fundamental 'non-political' human rights (the right to property, etc.), a concern which was not uppermost in the minds of those who constructed older models of democracy; (b) the idea that people-in-general, i.e. all men, have a natural right to govern themselves[7]; (c) the somewhat sceptical viewpoint that since one cannot define moral duties absolutely and universally, people should be governed (pragmatically) according to their own wishes[8]; (d) the tripartite 'balance of power' between the executive, legislative, and judicial branches, a creation of British ingenuity which was imitated in French and American models (Plato and Aristotle spoke of the possibility of a multipartite government, but not as a desideratum *in a democracy* for preventing a usurpation of power); and (e) the new idea that the fundamental ideals of democracy were appropriate for, and even eminently workable in, extremely large nations or centralised federations of multiple states.[9]

But at the time this modern version of 'democracy' was appearing, terminological problems had already reared their ugly heads – problems which to a great extent are still with us. The term 'democracy' in James Madison's day connoted radical egalitarianism, universal and *direct* participation of the citizenry in decision-making; in other words, a kind of *populism*, to be attained by applying some of the peculiar features from the Greek model in an idealistic fashion to an immensely larger populace. But respected thinkers such as Rousseau and Helvetius had said that this ideal sort of democracy could not exist in large states, and the inclination of American theoreticians such as Madison and Jefferson was to ask whether democracy was so 'ideal', after all, and to show how a government incorporating all that was best in democracy, and keeping itself as 'democratic' as possible, might be a definite improvement over the old ideal of democracy. At any rate, it became obvious to all the architects of the American 'experiment' that a democracy 'in a strict sense' was completely impractical and outmoded for a country like America. The only model that would do was that of a 'republic' – which in the American interpretation meant at least something like the Roman Republic which had a semblance of direct representation of the people through the 'popular assemblies' and an extremely indirect kind of participation in the aristocratic Roman senate.[10] Some type of indirect participation would be necessary in the American situation. The thing to do was to accept the idea of a republic in principle, and then increase popular participation and representation as much as possible. The result was that, in the early days after the American revolution, the new form of government was referred to with some exactitude as a 'democratic republic' or a 'representative democracy'. However, both terms, 'democracy' and 'republic', were used to designate a government which eschewed tyranny, and they were often utilised almost as synonyms, resulting in such confusions as Thomas Jefferson's statement that 'governments are more or less republican, as they have more or less the element of popular election and control in their composition'.[11] Jefferson uses the term 'republican' here and other places no doubt because of his opposition to any large-scale direct democracy,[12] but, strictly, the term 'democratic' would seem to make more sense in context.

As populations and democracies mushroomed in magnitude, the idea of 'direct democracy' became more and more impracticable, and the necessity for distinguishing 'direct' from 'representative' subsided. At the present time 'democracy' is synonymous with 'representative' or 'republican' government for both liberals and conservatives in 'mainstream' Western politics. The confusion of the terms 'democracy' and 'republic' in the United States even led once to an interesting court case in which a citizen of Oregon challenged his state in the Supreme Court for instituting direct referenda in opposition to the principles of 'republicanism', which (he objected) dictated an *in*direct form of representation.[13]

From this very terminological and conceptual confusion, however, we get a good idea of what is perhaps the main philosophical problem pertaining to the basic structure of a large democratic–republican government: *is the emphasis to be put on a broad-based popular participation in government, as direct as possible? or is the emphasis better placed on an indirect representation of the masses by a highly qualified and specialised élite?* Spectra of political opinion in many modern democracies have developed more or less along the lines of their response to this question, and all sorts of policy decisions are obviously affected by the stand one takes on this issue.

Let us take the United States as a test case: as long as we prescind from the notion of direct democracy and other characteristics which were more germane to the ancient model of democracy, the US will be found to have to some degree many of the basic characteristics which we referred to at the outset of this chapter as being pertinent to democracies in general. (Note that, at this point in our analysis of the meaning of democracy, 'democracy' has taken on the aspect of a genus, while 'direct democracy', or democracy proper, and 'republicanism', or 'representative democracy', are two species, both of which are best designated by their proper names, but may also be referred to correctly by their single generic designation.) But as 'American' democracy has evolved, it seems to have taken on the following individuating characteristics: (a) a new notion of representation, emphasising the fact that a man can not be bound legally by enactments of 'representatives' not subjected to his *vote* (this interpretation was originally designed, of course, to prevent any recurrence of the 'taxation without representation' and other abuses that had led the American colonies to rebel against Britain); (b) constitutional guarantees of liberty so sacrosanct and permanent that not even Congress can alter them fundamentally; (c) a positive (though by no means official or written) encouragement of intermediary organisations and interest groups – elements which Rousseau considered to be inimical to democracy[14]; and (d) a unique genre of élitism according to which the 'people' are to be trusted only as a kind of 'jury' for judging 'matters of fact' and the human character of those they choose to represent them in relatively clear-cut situations, but are thought to lack competence to make complex decisions on policy or persons[15] (even popular elections of presidents must be filtered through the elaborate mechanisms of the 'electoral college'). Such features of American democracy contrast rather remarkably with, for example, the guarantee of rights through specific legislation (rather than a Bill of Rights) and the close nexus between legislative and executive powers in the British model, the compromises between presidential and Cabinet government in the French model, the interplay of direct Canton democracy and representative city-democracy in Switzerland, etc.

In view of such multifarious departures from the ancient model, some writers have attempted to formulate a new definition of democracy general enough to accord with modern realities: Thus M. ten Hoor, recalling the ancient insight that democracies, unlike more autocratic governments, tend towards disorder, defines (modern) democracy (i.e. a democratic republic) as 'the continuous effort of the citizens through the medium of government to maintain society in a state of limited equilibrium between extremes of chaos and tyranny[16];

in other words to produce a 'middle road' between the extremes of absolutely independent self-centred individuals and no individual freedom at all. Joseph Schumpeter, with an eye to the issue of whether the extreme economic controls found in some modern socialist societies are compatible with democracy, formulates a definition of the 'democratic method' geared to accommodating many current forms of socialism: 'The democratic method is that institutional arrangement for arriving at political decisions in which individuals (i.e. the élite, and potential representatives of the people) acquire the power to decide by means of a competitive struggle for the people's vote.'[17] Both of these attempts at definition recognise the importance of the competition of special interest groups in democracy, but the latter definition emphasises the function of the competition among the politically élite as an element which keeps a modern democracy from ossifying and stagnating. Others seem to see a definite continuity of modern forms of democracy with ancient models and try to define democracy in more traditional terms. Dorothy Pickles in her book on democracy[18] requires for a democracy that there be a certain minimum of public participation in government combined with a certain minimum of government solicitation of public opinion, resulting in an ongoing 'dialogue' between rulers and ruled. In a similarly traditional vein Jack Lively pronounces a government 'democratic' just insofar as it approaches a 'situation of equality', which he defines as equal participation by all groups in public decision-making[19], and Michael Margolis states that a government which provides 'equal opportunity to participate in politics' is democratic.[20]

All in all, it is very important just how we *do* define democracy (whether or not we produce a formal and explicit verbal definition). If, for example, democracy is defined in antielitist or *populist* terms, critics who adhere to this definition will tend to look in very specific directions for what they consider to be possible or actual dangers to democracy: towards suspicious intellectualism and spurious bureaucratic 'expertise' and an overbearing technology which promotes the designs of the advocates of regimentation[21]; towards greater and greater concentration and centralisation of authority[22]; and towards the possibility of 'representative despotism', the possibility that a representative, even though subject to election and recall, may begin to operate contrary to the wishes of his constituency (e.g. by deferring to the wishes of special-interest groups who supply the funds without which it would be impossible for him to be elected again). On the other hand, if one defines democracy in *élitist* terms, the dangers begin to look quite different: one who is conscious of the importance of élites[23] in a democracy is most fearful of populist and anarchic trends, of the inevitable periodic appeals to decide important issues by popular referenda, and of the rather weak but not insignificant movements emerging now and then to try to inaugurate a system of direct democracy (something that now, for the first time in a large country, thanks to advances in technology, communications, electronic computers and 'two-way' television, will soon be quite *possible* to implement if there is any widespread and strong feeling in favour of it[24]). He is not at all secure about the much-heralded principle of 'one man, one vote', since he is quite aware (and feels it should be obvious to every thinking person) that many or perhaps even most of these equipollent votes will be cast by the incompetent, the uninformed, the relatively unconcerned or frivolous, or worst of all, those who stand to gain by a vote from which others will incur a loss. He also has reservations about the civil rights movement, not so much because of racism as because he knows it may provide the ultimate test as to whether the white élites can withstand mounting pressures from the unthinking *white* masses to take, contrary to their own principles, a simple promajority, antiminority, and, reductively, anti-élitist, stand.[25]

It may not be possible or even desirable to come up with a compromise definition of democracy which is neither populist-oriented (as, for example, Lively's) nor élitist-oriented (as, for example, Schumpeter's). Historically speaking, and in broader outline, such oscillation seems natural to Western democracy, trying to assimilate both its 'democratic' Greek heritage and its 'republican' Roman heritage. Some small consolation may be derived from reflecting on the fact that even Athenian democracy, on closer analysis, shows a parallel division of allegiance between two 'companionships' (the 'democratic club' and the oligarchic club'). So too, Roman republicanism, on closer analysis, shows an attempt to balance a commitment to popular assemblies with a commitment to higher echelon leadership. It is as if the Freudian 'band of brothers' which emerged after the 'primal crime' (in Western mythology) has been perpetually unable to decide whether it wanted specialised leadership (bringing with it the danger of reinstating the deposed father's iron grip) or broad participation of all in self-rule (in spite of doubts concerning whether all participants were equally capable, equally worthy, or equally interested).

NOTES

1. E.g. Robert Ardrey, in *The Social Contract* (NY: Atheneum, 1970) p. 100f; and as we shall see later in this chapter, M. ten Hoor would like to see a certain amount of 'chaos' as an ingredient for a viable definition of democracy.
2. This is the definition given by Plato, for example, in his *Republic*, Book VIII.
3. See Aristotle's *Politics* IV, 11, 1296a.
4. In ancient Sparta a council of 'ephors' was elected annually specifically to challenge and check the power of the Spartan kings. No doubt a similar check is necessary in a democracy – but with the opposite function: to check the power of the electorate. In view of this function (this seems to be the logic involved) those who are to fulfill it should be 'appointed' in some equitable fashion rather than elected.
5. Aristotle, however, did allow that democracy might work very well in a moderately large agricultural society, in which communication and ease of assembly was at a minimum. He observed that democracy might work better in such a situation than in cities, where maximal interaction, etc. might facilitate mob psychology and demogoguery. (See the *Politics*, VI, 4.) But it should be kept in mind that Aristotle did not favour democracy as a form of government and was simply searching for some variant less objectionable than the version he was familiar with.
6. Although these features have become explicit during a relatively brief period in modern times, there were long and laborious intellectual and attitudinal transitions in the Middle Ages which paved the way for most of the modern innovations, as Carl Friedrich points out in his excellent book, *Transcendent Justice: the Religious Dimensions of Constitution* (North Carolina: Duke University, 1964).
7. R. Wollheim, *Democracy*, op. cit., p. 227.
8. Ibid.
9. Thomas Jefferson, unlike many of his contemporaries, theorised that large countries would be more apt soil for democratic government than smaller ones, since it is generally much more difficult for any self-aggrandising faction to seize and misuse power in a large country than in a smaller one. See Adrienne Koch, *The Philosophy of Thomas Jefferson* (Chicago: Quadrangle, 1964) p. 151. James Madison in *The Federalist*, no. 10, also notes the tendency of 'pure democracies' (which can only exist amid small populations) to become unwieldy and self-destructive beause of the factionalism which is unavoidable in such compressed conditions.
10. This interpretation contrasts remarkably with the interpretation of Rousseau, who in his *Social Contract* (II, 6) defines a Republic as 'any state which is ruled by law', considers the term applicable to monarchies and aristocracies as well as democracies, and considers 'representative government', so extolled by the Americans, as conducive to the apathy, impotence, and even enslavement of its citizens.
11. From Jefferson's letter to John Taylor, in *The Writings of Thomas Jefferson*, A. E. Bergh ed. (Wash., DC: Jefferson Memorial Assn., 1903)

xv, 19. In this same letter, Jefferson defines a 'republic' as 'a government by its citizens in mass, acting directly and personally, according to rules established by the majority', and he laments the fact that the US government in some respects is deficient in the degree to which this popular control is exercised.

12. See A. Koch, *The Philosophy of Thomas Jefferson*, p. 152. See also Jefferson's letter of August 26, 1816, to Isaac H. Tiffany, in which, using the then much-utilised terms, 'republic' and 'democracy', more precisely than he usually does, he defines a democracy as 'the only pure republic, but impracticable beyond the limits of a town', and a republic as a government 'of the second grade of purity' which nevertheless is superior to democracy insofar as it 'may be exercised over any extent of country'. Thus Jefferson opposed direct democracy, not in principle, but because of its impracticability in larger countries. Jefferson in his presidency tried to insure an element of direct democracy through his 'Ward' system, but this system was, of course, subordinate to a fundamentally 'republican' form of government.
13. See *The Constitution of the United States: its Sources and Application*, by Thomas James Norton (NY: Committee for Constitutional Government, 1965) p. 168. The Supreme Court ruled that the case was a matter that only Congress could decide on, and thus was out of its jurisdiction.

    Initiatives and referenda are viewed by many as a way of increasing direct participation in government. The number of initiatives in the US in the 1970s has increased twofold at the state and local levels, as compared with the 1960s. The organisation, 'Initiative America', is currently trying to institutionalise initiatives on a national level.
14. Political scientists use various terms to refer to this phenomenon. Dye and Ziegler in *The Irony of Democracy* (NY: Wadsworth, 1970) call it 'pluralism' – a term which emphasises the interaction of multiple, often competing political élites; Pennock in *Democratic Political Theory* (Princeton University Press, 1979) refers to it as 'social pluralism', i.e. rule by various natural social, racial, occupational, religious, ethnic and sectional groupings; Dahl in *A Preface to Democratic Theory* calls it 'polyarchy', a term which he uses to emphasise the specifically social conflict of interests insofar as this affects the political realm; Frankel in the *Democratic Prospect* (NY: Harper, 1962) speaks of 'Politicking' as a necessity in the American system and ten Hoor in *Freedom Limited* refers to the necessity for conflict and compromise – necessities which are conditioned, of course, by the presence of multiple special interest groups, organisations and 'lobbies'.
15. See Dye and Ziegler, *The Irony of Democracy*, *passim*; Clinton Rossiter, *Alexander Hamilton and the Constitution* (NY: Harcourt, Brace & World, 1965) *passim*; Carl Friedrich, *Man and His Government* (NY: McGraw Hill, 1963), ch. XVII; and Koch, *The Philosophy of Thomas Jefferson*, p. 153.
16. *Freedom Limited*, p. 47.
17. *Capitalism, Socialism and Democracy* (NY: Harper, 1950) p. 269.
18. *Democracy* (Baltimore: Penguin, 1972) p. 13.
19. *Democracy* (NY: Capricorn, 1977) p. 2.

20. See *Viable Democracy* (NY: Penguin, 1979).
21. See Richard Goodwin, *The American Condition* (NY: Doubleday, 1974) *passim*; and Norman Brown, *Love's Body* (NY: Vintage, 1966) p. 9.
22. See Wm. Kornhauser, 'The Politics of Confrontation', in *The New American Revolution* (NY: Free Press, 1971).
23. The term 'élite' is used here in a wide sense. It includes industrialists, politicians, the educated, and military and religious leaders – 'the few' who exert control in the country as opposed to 'the many' who are controlled or apathetic to control.
24. Robt. Paul Wolff, offers a detailed proposal for 'Instant Direct Democracy' in *In Defense of Anarchism* (NY: Harper, 1970) pp. 34ff.
25. See Dye and Zeigler, *The Irony of Democracy*, ch. XII.

2 Equality

By nature, no one is a servant, no one a master. Nevertheless those who are better and more prudent have more 'rights' of an imperfect sort, than do others; and they also deserve greater respect and more prestigious offices.

But since there are no certain indications or criteria, by means of which it could be made apparent to all just *who* are better and more prudent; and those who are duller often pretend to have a superior prudence; and the worst men often put on such airs of honesty and goodness, that they can scarcely be differentiated from genuinely prudent and good men; – it is obvious that no one because of any claim he might have to prudence or goodness could arrogate any dominion over others, as long as these others were unwilling to accept that dominion. For this sort of 'right' would be the greatest possible hindrance to the common happiness.

Frances Hutcheson, *A Short Introduction to Moral Philosophy*

You will laugh at me, I know, ye bald-pated! – but, never mind, I will stick to my view: the fate of a subject, an individual, a personality is more important than the fate of the world and the weal of the Chinese emperor [viz., the Hegelian *Allgemeinheit*]. I am told: develop all the treasure of your spirit for the free self-enjoyment of the spirit, weep to console yourself, grieve to be glad, aspire to perfection, climb the top rung of the ladder of evolution and if you stumble, down you go, damn you – good riddance. No thank you, Yegor Fedorovich [a nickname for the German philosopher, Hegel], with all due respect to your philosophical philistinism, if I did succeed in reaching the top of the evolution ladder, I would demand even there an account from you of all the victims of the conditions of life and history, of all the victims of accident, superstition, the Inquisition, Phillip II, etc., etc.: otherwise I will throw myself headlong from the top rung. I will not have happiness if you gave it to me gratis unless I feel assured about every one of my blood brothers, the bone of my bone and flesh of my flesh.

V. G. Belinsky, letter to V. P. Botkin, 1 March 1841

> I do not believe in the doctrine of the greatest good of the greatest number. It means in its nakedness that in order to achieve the supposed good of 51 per cent the interest of 49 per cent may be, or rather should be sacrificed. It is a heartless doctrine and has done harm to humanity. *The only real*, dignified, human doctrine is the greatest good of all, and this can only be achieved by uttermost self-sacrifice.
>
> Mahatma Gandhi, quoted in *The Diary of Mahadev Desai*, vol. I

If one looks around his environment conscientiously and objectively, he must become convinced that, however the denizens of democracy arrived at the notion that 'all men are created equal', they did not come to this conclusion through any processes of systematic empirical observations or scientific induction of the ordinary sort. For any kind of objective perusal will show that men are basically, radically *un*equal in capacities and talents, attainments and accomplishments, as well as in wealth, physical attractiveness, health, and many other respects. He will perhaps not go so far as Aristotle, who theorised that some men were natural slaves, but he will probably feel inclined to find both irony and intimations of immense natural inequalities in Abraham Lincoln's dictum that freedom in our society (a) for some people means the freedom to do as they please with themselves and the product of their labour, but (b) for others means the freedom of *some* men to also do as they please with other men and the product of other men's labour. Whether or not one interprets this as a kind of master/slave dichotomy will depend, no doubt, on whether his definition of democracy is élitist or populist. The fact that many citizens of contemporary democracies are partially élitist is perhaps indicated by their acceptance of a parallel and long-recognised dichotomy implicit in the republican concept of 'representation'; namely, that (a) some are free to choose others to make decisions for them, while (b) others are free to make the decisions.

It may be precisely because of this almost self-evident *actual* inequality that some philosophers – e.g. Hobbes, and Rousseau – conceptualised man's *hypothetical* prepolitical origins as keynoted by equality: either men prior to the state are equally wild and aggressive (Hobbes), which would explain why political society is necessary in spite of the inequalities it brings; or equally good and innocent (Rousseau), which would lead us to maintain a constant vigilance against the possible corrupting influences of government; or equally free (Locke), which might explain why the present-day inherently unequal established societies must be decentralised and democratised (restored to the people), if they are to be vitalised.[1] Other thinkers less interested in hypothetical origins have conjectured that human equality consists right now in some primordial equality of needs,[2] or nature,[3] or moral sense,[4] or man's inability to really be sure that some men are better than others.[5]

In the French Revolution, which Hannah Arendt describes[6] as an egalitarian, 'compassionate' revolution, the main emphasis was on the Rousseauistic perspective: every man was equally good by nature, but this goodness had been marred by the artificial hierarchies of the social class system (the 'Estates') and could only be revitalised by dissolution of the latter. Later socialist and Marxist egalitarianism was characterised by a similar emphasis on the dissolution of class divisions, as a means of restoring persons to their natural unselfish and cooperative orientations.

In the non-socialist tradition, one of the most complicated 'proofs' that equality prevails among actually living men is offered by H. A. Myers, who reasons that since (a) each man is to himself the centre of the universe, therefore each man (b) must be 'equal to the great world of his own experience'; but (c) if all men are thus 'equal' to the world of experience, they must be equal among themselves, since 'men who are equal to the same thing, are equal to each other'.[7]

Contemporary writers, eschewing the somewhat metaphysical occupation of basing or 'deriving' the idea of equality from some 'natural' human condition, are often satisfied with merely describing and commenting on what they take to be the main empirically ascertainable forms of equality – equality of opportunity, equal rights and social equality.

Whether or not some condition of original 'natural' equality is envisioned, one may take equality as a future goal to be attained by gradual or radical means. This is equality in a 'prescriptive' sense,[8] i.e., a programme for assuring equality; it is more precisely a theory of 'equalisation'. Such 'prescriptive' equality seems to be the common denominator in futuristic utopian social visions, whether propounded in systematic philosophical theories or couched in fictional fantasies.[9]

Such multifarious modern secular thrusts towards equality seem to be products, corollaries or parallels, of religious beliefs which have developed in Christianity in the Western world. Early Christianity, in teaching that all men were the images of God and potential sons of God, and hence brothers, was a gradually equalising if not immediately democratising force in the world – insofar as the Church in most places throughout the dark ages and the middle ages was interested *ex officio* in validating equal entitlement of all men to certain basic and inalienable rights.[10] Luther, in teaching that all Christians were spiritually equal – equally priests, equally able to interpret Scripture – paved the way for Thomas Muntzer's somewhat socialistic theology which played a part in instigating the Peasants' revolt. It is interesting to note that Luther himself, when he saw some of the radical effects his teachings were having on the social order, began to modify his initial teachings somewhat. After the Peasants' Revolt he began to make a distinction between 'true Christians' and 'nominal Christians' – which was a return to élitism, if not to hierarchy in the Catholic sense. Similar developments took place in Calvinism. One might have thought that Calvin's extreme emphasis on the equal depravity of all men might be an incentive to egalitarianism. But the Calvinists, like Luther, soon found ways of distinguishing the elect from the damned, and correspondingly élitist socio-political structures seemed to be the most compatible with Calvinism.

In a way, Calvinism is the religious counterpart of the Hobbesian view of the original state of man. Insofar as Hobbes' theory led to a justification of monarchy and Calvinism seemed most adaptable to conservative forms of government, one might speculate that there is a predictable positive correspondence between a theory which views man in his original state as basically misdirected or bad, and various positions which are at the 'conservative' extremes of the political spectrum. If Pastore's thesis is correct that conservative political attitudes tend to correlate positively with a dim view of the basic worth of the average man (which leads them into élitism),[11] the converse may also be true – that such a dim view would tend to correlate positively with conservatism – although the latter thesis would not follow necessarily from Pastore's thesis.[12]

If the Calvinists were the Protestant conservatives, the Levellers in England were the Protestant liberals. Starting with the premise that all men had equal moral capacities, the Levellers became articulate spokesmen for what in their time were extremely liberal 'planks' – equal opportunity for all, and a kind of politico-economic *laissez-faire*. The logical conclusion of such socio-theological gravitation was no doubt epitomised in another English sect pejoratively called the 'Diggers', which practised a form of religious communism inspired by the theological views of Muntzer.

According to Lakoff,[13] G. W. F. Hegel in philosophy supplied the intellectual bridge from the religious socialism of groups like the

Diggers to the completely secularised socialism of Marx and Engels. Hegel, by impugning the Christian idea of a transcendent God and an afterlife, and de-mystifying the meaning of God's 'incarnation' in favour of an immanent spiritual unity of mankind – supplied the logical groundwork for the total dedication to 'immanent' human concerns and to the total unity of mankind, which is the theme of Marxian socialism. In a way, the Marxian solution marks the ultimate apotheosis of the humanism of the Enlightenment, which had aimed at replacing the superstitions, dogmas and rituals of the Church with a science of society, an ideology of unlimited social progress, and the institutionalisation of human care and concern for one's fellow.

As has already been indicated, the great egalitarian movements in eighteenth-century France and in the rise of nineteenth-century socialism seemed to equate equality with the dissolution of all social or socioeconomic distinctions. It must be emphasised that it was this objective that was primary, while the attainment of economic equality was secondary. Thus aside from Robespierre and his Jacobin confederates, most Frenchmen, even if dedicated to the abolition of class distinctions, were not similarly dedicated to the attainment of economic equality. And Marx and Engels, although they insisted on the seizure by the proletariat of all property and capital geared specifically to social or industrial uses, accepted the necessity for the perdurance of some differences in property holdings, income, etc. even after the advent of communism had overthrown the situation of distinction and alienation that had existed between the proletariat and bourgeoisie. However, in both cases, questions about economic equality eventually turned out to be unavoidable and even paramount. In the aftermath of the French Revolution, when titles and concomitant rights and privileges were no longer inheritable, it soon became apparent to the *citoyens* that property was the only thing left that *could* be inherited. Thus property differences were augmented rather than bridged. More recent social experiments in the obliteration of class differences have not been notably more successful in overcoming economic gaps. For example, as Milovan Djilas has pointed out,[14] in Marxism as actually practiced abolition of the old class system has resulted in a 'new class' with privileges of ownership and consumption largely proportionate to one's status in the communist hierarchies – so that wealth here, as in capitalism, supplies a useful 'rule of thumb' for determining who is indeed who.

Of course, there have been some social experiments which have aimed more directly than Leninist Marxism at the obliteration of economic inequalities. But such attempts at economic equalisation, from the pathfinding socialism of Francois Babeuf in 1795–96 to the more recent Cambodian experiments, have led to ironical socio-political consequences: to strive seriously for this ideal in its quasi-mathematical perfection, means that almost all the benefits of a highly diversified modern civilisation have to be sacrificed. The 'faithful' who survive the more extreme socialist revolutions have very little to share with one another except their own undifferentiated sameness, and even that in limited amounts.

* * *

The reader will recall that earlier in this chapter we spoke of attempts to trace the notion of equality philosophically to certain pivotal, paradigmatic or primordial types or states of equality, among which we included (1) the idea that in the 'beginning'[15] men were fundamentally equal, and (2) the notion that there is some ultimate future state of equality towards which we are heading, or should head. Before leaving the subject of equality, it behooves us to re-examine these positions in the light of modern science.

1 (a)

The American Declaration of Independence refers to the 'self-evident' truth that 'all men are created equal'. This, of course, could not be self-evident to one who did not believe at all in creation (by God). Subsequent to the ascendancy of the theory of evolution to the place of honour in modern science, atheists and even many Christians no longer believe in the creation of man, in the usual sense. Formerly the notion that all men had been created by God (the Father) was, as it were, a premise leading to the conclusion that all men were basically brothers (sons of God) – a conclusion that was a strong buttress for the cause of political equality in the world. Now, with evolution, that buttress has been removed. Men (even if they believe evolution is something established by God, or even identical with God) are not likely, at least at present, to look upon the impersonal processes of evolution with feelings of filial love and communal belongingness. Is there any sense in which evolution might substitute (in the theoretical realm) for the boon to equality previously furnished by creationism? There is one way, but it is a long shot: the idea of the basic unity of a species (witness the case of many herd animals) could be a powerful incentive to sentiments of fraternity or identification with group interests[16] *provided that* 'something happened' to make this idea of species-unity more forcible and compelling. Some of the possibilities are already familiar to readers of science fiction: a struggle for survival with certain species of animals or plants; war with species from some other planet; world-wide concerted efforts to join against some common impersonal enemy (e.g. pollution, or the possibility of nuclear destruction or evil itself); or concerted international efforts to explore and conquer the 'unknown horizons' of outer space. Short of such outside possibilities, it would seem impossible to create the conditions for the emotional unity that would render the 'brotherhood of men' a conclusion from new self-evident premises.

(b) 'Social contract' theories have to be re-examined in the light of current anthropological findings concerning the state of primitive men. It is no longer necessary to speak merely hypothetically about man's original state, because the science of anthropology does give us some concrete facts (still needing to be sorted out and interpreted) about primitive human conditions. Robert Ardrey, in *The Social Contract*, challenges proponents of such theories to take into account an actual fact about the pre-historical existence of men, which anthropology has been able to verify: that our ancestors were instinctively aggressive and always unequal.[17] Ardrey, accepting original inequality as a fact, suggests that we should simply try to provide a minimum equality of opportunity to make sure that men, like animals, will be able to affirm their individuality and distinguish themselves: 'every vertebrate born, excepting only in a few rare species, is granted equal opportunity to display his genius or make a fool out of himself'. Ardrey's criticisms[18] might provide a useful counterbalance to a social contract theory which presumed an original, common innocence or goodness of men (such as Rousseau's), and even provoke a re-examination of a contrary social contract theory which presumed men were all wild and aggressive (such as Hobbes'). However, in regard to the latter, it should be noted that, whereas Hobbes concluded from the common condition of wildness that all men were in an 'equal' state, Ardrey sees this same common aggressiveness as concomitant to and perhaps even spurred on by a wide variety of individual differences or inequalities. Even if Ardrey is correct, he unintentionally begs the question: which came first, the aggressiveness or the inequality? Contemporary anthropology might lead us to hypothesise an interesting linkage, according to which a latent aggressiveness can be spurred on by inequalities, but may also be responsible for creating these inequalities in the first place. The cause of equality will be perhaps best served by a recognition of a bidirectional, reciprocal causality between both factors, aggression and inequality.

2 The Marxians and utopian socialists would like us to view equality as a *terminus ad quem* towards which men are inexorably heading by historical or dialectical processes, and which may or may not be a return to some primitive state or *terminus a quo*. The theory of evolution, if interpreted in terms of random 'natural selection' and 'survival of the fittest', is individualistic in its thrust, and would seem to place in doubt any projected utopian future of idyllic unity. But some evolutionists, in particular Teilhard de Chardin, extrapolate the future of evolution in terms of some higher super-organic unity, characterised by an extraordinarily intensified sense of unity ('collective consciousness'), and an inexorable drift towards world government.[19] Teilhard makes serious efforts to show that such communal developments would not impugn or submerge individuality. Teilhard thus extolls the 'impossible ideal', the ideal of maximal differentiation combined with maximal unity – such as obtains in organisms and would obtain in an advanced stage of development of the 'super-organism' of the human species. This theory has been echoed sympathetically by Julian Huxley, Lewis Thomas the biologist, and Theodosius Dobzbansky the geneticist. A theory about the future, of course, is only a probable projection based on an assessment of present facts and tendencies, and may also be heavily influenced by one's socio-political biases, as Bethell shows in his article.[20] But at the very least, Teilhard's theory impells us to ask: is it not an indubitable fact that man's socio-cultural evolution and history has led so far to greater and greater differentiation and individuation? and if this is the case, could we seriously expect evolution to reverse itself, as it were, and to move now monochromatically in the direction of homogeneity and equalisation?[21]

Whether we approach our interpretation of equality from the point of view of Hobbes or Jefferson or Marx or from some other scientific or philosophical viewpoint, there is one ever-present danger that must be avoided: that we might try to apply 'equality', an idea taken over from mathematics, in a mathematical or quasi-mathematical fashion. Mathematically, it seems to be 'equality' when the rich man is fined the same as the poor man; when a complex, clever and eloquent political figure is tried by a jury of ordinary citizens chosen after all the professional or educated or influential people (who might be able to best understand the complexities and nuances of what the politician has been doing) have been excused from jury duty; when teenagers with no academic interest or ability are nevertheless given an academic education to spare them the social opprobrium of going to a technical or commercial school; when voters with an enormous stake in the outcome of a particular referendum are given the same vote (no more, no less) as those who are completely unconcerned about this particular issue; when a company that has consistently and as a matter of policy denied promotion and pay rises to minorities and women decides, when that policy is contested, to set matters right by simply beginning to apply the same criteria for promotion and merit pay increases to all, 'starting today', and forgetting about the past. Such practices may be considered approximations to equality, by people who gravitate towards solutions based on simple mathematics; but they have little relationship to bona fide political equality, which must take into account immensely complex historical or social contexts, and which involves all kinds of individual and social 'relativities'.

Clearly, none of the positions discussed prove definitively that equality ever has existed, exists now, or ever can exist in mankind. But such a demonstration is unimportant for promoting the cause of equality in the world. This latter seems to be the result primarily of a *belief* in the basic equality of man (perhaps nourished by some philosophical or religious theory about original human equality) and/or a *willingness* (perhaps nourished by some utopian or religious ideal of a better, less selfishly motivated society) to work for the eventual 'equalisation' of mankind in important respects.[22] Many of those who have this willingness and/or that belief may be expected to gravitate towards the side of equality in time of class confrontation or crisis, even though they may happen to have advantages and privileges which would have to be sacrificed to some extent in the name of equality.

NOTES

1. For representative statements of these 'state of nature' theories see e.g. Hobbes' *Leviathan*, I, 3; *Locke's Second Treatise on Government*, VX, 123; and Rousseau's *A Discourse on the Origins of Inequality*, First Part.
2. Thomas Jefferson grounded his notion of 'equal rights' in man's basic need for life, for sustenance of life, for freedom of motion, for thought and the expression of thought. Koch, *The Philosophy of Thomas Jefferson*, pp. 143–4.
3. Emerson, for example, thought that all men shared one and the same universal nature and, grasping this fact intuitively, would be led to accept the basic equality of all men. See H. A. Myers, *Are Men Equal?* (NY: Great Seal Books, 1963).
4. The Scottish philosopher, Francis Hutcheson (1694–1746) was the first philosopher to elaborate in his *Short Introduction to Moral Philosophy* and elsewhere a theory of social equality based on the equal possession by all men of a 'moral sense'. This theory found sympathetic reverberations in Adam Ferguson, Adam Smith and David Hume, and has been periodically resuscitated by other writers since that time. In the nineteenth century, Leonard Nelson (1882–1927) derived equality from man's orientation towards ethical norms, which do not admit of any discrimination in their application (see Brecht, *Political Theory*, pp. 307–8).
5. Carl Cohen, 'The Justification of Democracy', in *The Monist*, LVI, 1, Jan. 1971, p. 25.
6. See Arendt's *On Revolution* (NY: Viking, 1965) ch. 2.
7. *Are Men Equal?* p. 32.
8. See R. M. Hutchins, M. J. Adler, and O. Bird, 'The Idea of Equality', in *The Great Ideas Today* (Chicago: Encyclopedia Brittanica, 1968).
9. In America, a nineteenth-century novelist with socialist leanings, Edward Bellamy, wrote an enormously successful futuristic novel entitled *Looking Backward, 2000–1888*, which depicted America in the year 2000 with all wealth evenly distributed by means of a 'credit card' system by which one is simply given whatever he needs.
10. Carl Friedrich, in *Transcendent Justice* (NC: Duke University, 1964) ascribes this tendency, which he considers the basis of 'constitutionalism', almost wholly to the Church, and not to Greek democracy or Roman republicanism, which granted only certain rights affecting political participation.
11. See Nicholas Pastore, *The Nature-Nurture Controversy* (NY: King Crown, 1949) p. 15. Pastore tries to show that political conservatism also correlates positively with an attitude favouring 'hereditarianism', while liberal views correlate both with a basic optimism about the average man along with an 'environmentalist' approach to the study of man. Lakoff in *Equality in Political Philosophy*, pp. 8–11, develops the similar thesis that political conservatism correlates with a rather negative view on equality, while socialists are the paradigmatic proponents of equality. 'Liberalism' is defined by Lakoff as a middle position between the two extremes.

12. For a further discussion of Pastore's thesis and its cultural contexts, see H. Kainz, *The Philosophy of Man, Revisited: a New Introduction to Some Perennial Issues* (Tuscaloosa: University of Alabama Press, 1981) ch. 3.
13. *Equality in Political Philosophy*, p. 196.
14. In *The New Class* (NY: Praeger, 1957).
15. Some 'social contract' theorists, e.g. Hugo Grotius, were concerned with the initial state of man in a historical sense. Others, e.g. Rousseau, simply tried to present a hypothesis concerning what mankind would be like if we could abstract from the existence of a fully formed political society. In this latter case, the original 'state of nature' is prior to the state not temporally but intellectually.
16. A. A. Myers in *Are Men Equal?* p. 107, theorises that Darwinism, in supposing the basic unity of all members of the species *homo sapiens*, would be an incentive to sentiments of equality, if it were not for the fact that Darwin himself, as well as other exponents of evolutionism such as Spencer, did not choose to interpret 'the facts' in this way. Tom Bethel, in 'Burning Darwin to Save Marx', *Harper's*, Dec. 1978, shows that attempts have indeed been made continually to present evolution in a more egalitarian, less Darwinian–Spencerian fashion, and portrays contemporary 'socio-biology' as an unsuccessful attempt of Darwinians to compromise with the egalitarians by pointing to the 'selfish *gene*' as the culprit for making otherwise altruistic humans do some competitive things in spite of themselves.
17. Robert Wokler, in 'Perfectible Apes in Decadent Cultures: Rousseau's Anthropology Revisited', in *Daedalus*, 107, 3 Summer, 1978, suggests that Ardrey's critique of Rousseau is invalid because Ardrey (and interpreters of Rousseau in general) have failed to realise that Rousseau's 'savage man', was an *orangutan*. Thus Ardrey's criticism that Rousseau's social contract was constructed by 'fallen angels', while his own social contract is an agreement between 'risen apes' is wide of the mark. 'In fact,' says Wokler, 'there are no angels of any sort in Rousseau's state of nature, and Ardrey ought to have perceived that, according to Rousseau, men are actually fallen apes . . .' (p. 124). Since orangutans are not notably aggressive, a social contract based on the orangutan origins of men would have to be more like the theory proposed by Rousseau than that propounded by Ardrey.

    The theory of innate human aggressivity has been challenged recently by the anthropologist, Richard Leakey in *Origins* (NY: Dutton, 1978) ch. 9, and the sociobiologist Edward O. Wilson in *Sociobiology: the New Synthesis* (Cambridge, Mass.: Harvard University Press, 1975) ch. 5. But neither author claims man is innately altruistic.
18. Op. cit. (NY: Atheneum, 1970) p. 95ff.
19. See Pierre Teilhard de Chardin, *The Phenomenon of Man*, IV, 2.
20. See note 16.
21. For a fuller discussion of the variety of options available now under the rubric of 'socio-cultural evolution', see H. Kainz, *The Philosophy of Man, Revisited: a New Look at Some Perennial Issues* (Tuscaloosa: University of Alabama Press, 1981) ch. 5.
22. Of this latter sort is the approach to equality advocated by Pragmatism,

which, eschewing all questions about the natural equality of men, justifies equality simply on the basis of the conceivable effects it is likely to have. See G. W. Mortimore, 'An Ideal of Equality', in *Mind*, LXXVII, 1968.

3 Equality *vs.* Liberty?

Today, when only the herd animal is honoured and dispenses honor . . . – is greatness possible?

Friedrich Nietzsche, *Beyond Good and Evil*

In Britain, the Labour party finds itself in danger of being torn asunder by the demands of some to equalize and of others to give greater liberty to enterprisers. In the United States your liberty to contribute without limit to the campaign of your favorite candidate and his liberty to spend must contend with the ideal of equality of opportunity in the electoral race. The liberty of free association, for example, in schools, clubs, and the like, confronts the egalitarian ideal of integration. And again the ideal of equal access to medical treatment finds itself in tension with the liberty of the individual to select his or her own doctor.

J. Roland Pennock, *Democratic Political Theory*

[After the Second World War] the Russian and American peoples were ill equipped for understanding each other. The Americans saw their *summum bonum* in a personal liberty which they rather oddly identified with equality, whereas the Russian Communist dominant minority saw their *summum bonum* in a theoretical equality which they still more oddly identified with liberty.

Arnold Toynbee, *A Study of History*

THE SOURCE OF CONFLICT

If we were asked to generalise on the various ideas and movements we have just discussed under the rubric of 'equality', we would have to say that they represent a concerted and persistent thrust, violent or gradual, towards the dissolution of whatever are considered to be the more egregious class distinctions, and a concomitant and apparently inseparable effort to socially orchestrate a broader distribution of material possessions. The simultaneous (and sometimes coterminous or collocated) movements toward *liberty*, on the other hand, march to the sound of a different drummer. Like Hobbes they may define liberty as the right to preserve one's own nature and do what they want without unnecessary obstacles, or like Locke they may add the stipulation that what they want to do should be in accord with the laws of nature or morality, or like Mill they may stipulate that others not be harmed. But the emphasis is generally on a lack of restriction in doing what one wants or considers to be right.

As we saw in Chapter 1, some writers, including the English political theoretician, Jack Lively, prefer to define democracy in terms of some form of equality. Others, such as the American theorist, Carl Cohen, choose to emphasise liberty.[1] Sometimes the apparent divergence here is no more than a mild difference of emphasis, but sometimes strong ideological disparities make their appearance. For some champions of egalitarianism, from the Roosevelt-era liberals to the socialists, the proponent of individualism and 'liberty', usually wearing the attire of the conservative or the 'middle-of-the-roader', will amount to a veritable chief antagonist in the drama of democracy. And it is taken as an almost self-evident truth among some political theorists that liberty and equality are opposed values: in so far as one bends towards one of these values (they tell us) he distances himself from the other, although there may be some ideal (and largely unattainable) point at which both values converge.[2]

One of the most eloquent spokesmen for the preservation of 'liberty' from the threatening currents of equality was the aristocratic Frenchman Alexis de Tocqueville, whose classic *Democracy in America* (1835) can be considered a long and elaborate series of variations on this single theme: that the currents of egalitarian democracy are irresistible features of the (then current) evolution of society, but a potential menace to the values of freedom and individual excellence which are so dear to aristocratic Europeans. In the United States (considered by Tocqueville to be the epitome of such egalitarianism), there was unfortunately little appreciation of, or sympathy for, such 'aristocratic' values. In spite of innumerable positive features which de Tocqueville discerned in the American 'experiment', he departed from American shores with an overall impression that the 'levelling' tendencies of democracy would create a mediocre, materialistic, super-conforming populace with only a faint trace of an idea of what it means to live and breathe freedom. Many of de Tocqueville's predictions about America have turned out to be perceptive, e.g. that

America would eventually share world domination with Russia[3]; but on other points he seems to have been very wide of the mark, e.g. in his contention that American egalitarianism would characteristically produce mediocre leaders – an observation that does not seem to be borne out, if we compare the history of American leadership with European leadership.[4]

Hannah Arendt[5] presents us with an America very different from Tocqueville's: in Arent's estimation, it was precisely the emphasis on liberty rather than equality that justified, and guaranteed the success of, the American Revolution and the *novus ordo saeculorum* which it inaugurated. The French Revolution, on the other hand, in spite of its lip-service to *liberté*, was so overly enamoured of *égalité* that the revolution was bogged down in sentimentality and insoluble problems, and eventually proved abortive.

Who is right, Arendt or Tocqueville? Actually, they are both right, and their apparent disagreement only serves to accentuate the relativity of both liberty and equality: from the vantage point of the aristocratic Tocqueville living in the post-Napoleonic 'restoration' at a time when socialist experiments were esoteric or utopian with generally little broad public support, the United States loomed as the foremost example of the egalitarian philosophy. Because of historical contingencies – the then-recent revolution, the existence of a vast frontier, the national and ethnic pluralism and tolerance which characterised it – America simply was at that time the standard-bearer for the principle of equality, so much so that the neo-aristocratic or élitist trends in the US were hard to discern amidst all the bustle (Tocqueville did discern some of these, but saw them as relatively subordinate to the mainstream tendencies.)

From Arendt's vantage point in time, on the other hand, it became clear that socialism and Marxism had become the true heirs to the idealistic egalitarian aspirations of Robespierre, the Jacobins, Babeuf, etc. But it should be noticed that both Tocqueville and Arendt in their own separate ways are indicating intimations of incompatibility between egalitarianism and libertarianism.

British thinkers, such as Edmund Burke, J. S. Mill and Herbert Spencer, expressed similar sentiments concerning the question of the compatibility of egalitarian and libertarian democracy. Mill, in particular, took Tocqueville's criticisms to heart, and lamented a conformism and a tendency to stifle minority opinions among the proponents of equality. In his essay, *On Liberty* (1859), he expressed the basic 'libertarian' principle that 'the sole end for which mankind are warranted, individually or collectively, in interfering with the liberty of action of any of their number, is self-protection'.[6] This concept of liberty, as the capability of disposing of oneself and one's labour without impediment, is common to all of the advocates of liberty we have mentioned – except that for Tocqueville, 'liberty' is especially connected with creative excellence and a sense of honour. Mill insisted that, if equality was not to be counterproductive, it would have to flourish strictly within the limits of this libertarian principle. Mill finally modified these sentiments somewhat in what he called the 'third stage' of his career as a political economist, when he took an interest in socialism and edged towards socialist solutions, without actually embracing a 'socialist's socialism' (Mill still voiced reservations about the social and political consciousness of the working class, expressed fears about the possible effects of socialist controls on individual liberty, and insisted that social welfare benefits should not be distributed to those who were lazy).

A more recent spokesman in favour of liberty in preference to equality is Milton Friedman, who in his *Capitalism and Freedom* develops from many directions the thesis that, if we understand equality as *material* equality (as distinguished from equality of opportunity and equality of treatment under the law), then equality is *contrary to* what he calls 'liberalism', i.e. the furtherance of liberty.[7]

This distinction is very important because it seems to pinpoint the main, although often implicit, objection to equality voiced by Mill, Spencer, and others who did not write from a specifically economic point of view; and it brings to a head a problem that we have already seen looming large in Chapter 2: theoretically, by a process of abstraction it is quite possible to consider the other aspects of equality in isolation from the economic aspects. We can think about an individual in abject poverty who has nothing but similarly poor and abject friends and acquaintances as being (let us say) quite talented and able to make use of all kinds of educational resources (in his spare time, after work) in the name of 'equal opportunity'; and in the name of 'equal rights' as being eligible for adequate and complete legal representation (if he can raise the bail to look for a lawyer), in case he is accused of a crime. In some cases it actually works out this way. And from a Spencerian–Darwinistic point of view, this is the way that evolution will bring the 'cream of the cream' – those who ought to survive – to the top. But it takes no great knowledge of mathematical statistics to realise that there are tremendous odds against even a talented, aggressive and even potentially virtuous individual (if he can remain patient to the end) ever attaining these other types of equality without some minimal economic equality. This point has been argued by many 'liberal' writers at length, so there is no need to dwell on it here. Suffice it to say that the idea that all individuals should be *equally* entitled to some basic *material* prerequisites in life seems to be the crux of libertarian distrust of equality. Even Tocqueville, in his frequently recurring remarks about the 'materialism' of the Americans or the widespread possession among them of objects of only middling quality, seems to have this at least in the back of his mind. As E. F. Carritt observes, 'the main fear of the prominent thinkers who have contrasted liberty so glowingly with equality seems to be precisely that political egalitarianism would promote . . . *economic equality* – which they feel to be quite incompatible with their own liberty'.[8] For it seems naïve to expect that multitudes of abject people could be brought up to, and preserved in, adequate living standards without some expropriation, albeit through 'peaceful' means (i.e., taxation), of the relatively *wealthy*; or that this expropriation would not, to a greater or lesser extent, limit the *liberty* of the relatively wealthy. Rousseau, a philosopher of equality, seemed to minimise the importance of these consequences when he stated that without a total equality and a total dedication of each member of the community to the welfare of the others, there could not be (universal) freedom.[9] Critics of Rousseau, seeing the implications of this idea, have claimed that Rousseau's 'social contract' was the forerunner of totalitarianism (insofar as it offered a pretext for imposing a harsh, putative 'General Will' in contravention to the empirical 'Will of All'). There is some plausibility in this claim, since Rousseau allowed that at least in the case of very large states a dictatorship would probably be necessary to insure social unity – involving a sacrifice of 'natural liberty' for the 'moral liberty' that is synonymous with 'equality before the law'. This, of course, must be taken in the context of Rousseau's general opposition to large states. But it serves to highlight the truth that it is possible to work for the extension of equality in a completely abstract sense, which involves the sacrifice of liberty. If, under a rigid dictatorship, all class differences were obliterated and all surplus wealth were expropriated and distrubuted among the underprivileged, a state of universal economic equality, and perhaps even equality under (dictatorial, martial) law might result at least for a time, but the liberty to use, trade, and multiply the possessions thus distributed would be singularly absent. Thus the fact that all men were *equal* would not mean they were free, just as (as Aristotle observed long ago) the fact that all men were 'equally' free would not necessarily mean that they were equal in other respects. But such reflections should simply put us on our guard against dangerous abstractions. In concrete states, even in large ones, it should be possible by means of a sacrifice of excess wealth, excessive privilege, and some of the more exotic and unessential liberties, to attain more than a modicum of equality *and* liberty for the vast majority (short of utopianism, one can never say 'all').

This latter is precisely a point on which some libertarians are most sensitive. They do not seem to *believe* that even a modicum of liberty is something that could possibly be enjoyed 'equally' by *most* men. As Aptheker observes, the great champions of freedom in history have characteristically drawn sharp limits as to the potential extensivity of this freedom. John Milton drew the limits short of the Papists, Jefferson excluded women and Tories in his concept of political freedom, and Mill would exclude non-taxpayers and the uneducated.[10] We might add that conservative political economists like Milton Friedman, in their apparent willingness to extend liberty to all but not equality, are in reality withholding liberty also, since the two values cannot be completely separated except only in the mind or on paper. It is possible to be free with minimal wherewithal and to be 'more equal than others' with minimal liberty, but it is not possible to be free without minimal equality.

G. W. F. Hegel (1770–1831), who was neither a libertarian nor a proponent of equality, observed in several places that the whole thrust of history seemed to be towards wider and wider participation in freedom.[11] In the beginning, he tells us, only one man was free – the despot or monarch; then gradually the aristocrat and nobles came to share some of the power and freedom among themselves; and in modern times the same inestimable benefits are being shared by ordinary people (meaning for Hegel primarily the middle class). But Hegel also indulges himself in the psychological–metaphysical insight that a relationship to *property* is an indispensable prerequisite for the attainment of a free personality,[12] without drawing any logical connection between property and freedom. It was up to Hegel's disciple, Marx, to put these two ideas together and conclude in his dialectical political economics that universal freedom is impossible without a transcendence of capitalist economic relations and a consequent reappropriation of property. And to complete the task thoroughly, Marx not only (unlike Hegel) includes the lower-class 'proletariat' in his projections of freedom and equality, but proposes reversing the whole class structure and putting the proletariat at the top – constituting what an aristocrat might call a 'negative' or inverted aristocracy.

Thus Marx, in a style reminiscent of Jesus' promise that 'the poor will possess the earth' (presumably in the next life), projects a similar destiny for the proletariat (but definitely on earth, and in this mortal life). Perhaps it is regrettable that Marx had to make such a strong statement and even (by advocating a dictatorship of the proletariat, etc.) seemingly ignore values of liberty in the name of equality. Long before Marx, Plato had made the potentially radical statement that a just and stable society cannot exist where there are extremes of poverty and wealth, and Aristotle attributed the existence of crime and violence in a society (certainly a restriction on everyone's liberty) to the pockets of poverty which it tolerated and perpetuated – and neither one of them were branded as revolutionaries. But, of course, these ancient social observations were but parenthetical points in the context of what were considered much more substantial political observations, and no one paid much attention to them. If Marx, who 'specialised' in social philosophising, had been similarly moderate and to the point, his fate might have been being ignored *in toto*.

On the other hand, Marx's prescription of communism as the lever for bringing about absolute equality – and, *ipso facto*, fulfillment and freedom – is too oversimplified a solution to be truly democratic. In order to implement communism with a bona fide, stable equality in a concrete, traditionally democratic (i.e. non-dictatorial) framework, much more than the Marxian revolutionary formulas would be required. In order for those making the distribution of goods in a communistic society to determine as exactly as possible the needs of all, it would be necessary to have the fullest possible contact with individuals to learn of their specific needs; and, optimally, it would be wise to let them as far as possible determine their *own* needs (otherwise they will be unlikely to use efficiently what is given to them, and waste will result). Then again, in implementing communism, one would not be so naïve as to exact the same sort and amount of work from all individuals: he would adopt the Marxian maxim, 'from each according to his ability'. But the best way to determine the strengths and abilities of persons is to allow maximum range for experimentation, mobility, failure, re-education, even periodic inactivity – all of which runs contrary to the goal of equal input in a communistic society, and is embarrassingly close to the ideals of a democratic or libertarian society.

It would be possible, perhaps to achieve agreement, even among many conservative 'libertarian' elements, that some basic minimum standards for sustaining life should be applied to all men equally. Even the most inveterate sceptic concerning equality – if he is faced point-blank with a clear indication that his position, carried to its logical conclusion, would result in death or degredation for such-and-such specific individuals – might make some concessions to equality in the name of humanitarianism or at least the spirit of compromise. But it is when we go beyond this 'bare minimum' of material equality to try to *assure* equality of opportunity, etc., as well as freedom, that the disagreements as well as the complexities arise in full force. Suffice it to say that no one charismatic leader, and no one political or politico-economic theory is capable of dealing with such complexities. Our main 'problem' in the past has been perhaps a 'second-order' problem: the very human tendency to rely on simple or one-sided solutions in response to enormously complicated and multi-faceted problems.[13] The egalitarian who realises the harmful effects that, e.g. free competition is having on human equality, may hope to further the equality by doing away with the competition; but he must reach a certain point of regulation where further restriction of competition will do away with *meaningful* equality and result in something like Rousseau's 'natural man', whose relative innocence results from the lack of opportunity to develop his natural talents or fulfil long-range goals.[14] On the other hand, our 'libertarian', who realises only too well the dangers of regimentation and 'levelling', would hope to serve the cause of freedom by doing away with all 'artificial' diverting of what should be his personal rewards to the 'undeserving'; but in doing this beyond a certain point will further a situation reminiscent of that peculiarly Hobbesian state of nature in which 'the war of all against all' neutralises even the supposedly unrestricted liberty which each individual possesses.

THE CONTEMPORARY DEBATE

On both the theoretical and practical levels, we encounter conflicts, or apparent conflicts, between liberty and equality. Aware of the immense implications of this conflict for contemporary political development and progress, some concerned philosophers have tried to act as mediators in the conflict. John Rawls' *A Theory of Justice*[15] is one of the most notable attempts in that direction in recent years. Rawls tries to avoid, on the one hand, the pseudo-egalitarianism of classical utilitarianism, which is oriented towards maximising one's personal advantage under the cover of 'working for the greatest happiness of the greatest number (to which, I the utilitarian, just happen to belong!)',[16] and, on the other hand, the extreme conservative 'libertarian' position which, in the name of 'liberty', embraces the overtly egoistic thesis that 'everyone is permitted to advance his interests as he pleases'.[17] In attempting to avoid these extremes, Rawls introduces an ingenious philosophical device, called the 'veil of ignorance', which is reminiscent of Rene Descartes' famous 'methodological doubt',[18] and Edmund Husserl's 'phenomenological epoche'.[19] Just as Descartes tries to achieve certitude about reality by subjecting basic accepted realities to searing and searching doubt to see what, if anything, remains unscathed, and thus indubitably certain; and just as Husserl attempts in a similar vein to attain certitude about the fundamental ideal or 'eidetic' structures that influence the horizons of our consciousness, by subjecting the 'natural world' to a temporary methodological–phenomological suspension (or 'epoche'), so also Rawls devises the 'veil of ignorance' as a tactical procedure geared to producing maximum certainty regarding the basic principle or principles of justice which should prevail.[20] Rawls asks us to temporarily and methodologically suspend all our knowledge of our present position in society, our privileges, our physical, psychological and intellectual assets, so as to place ourselves (mentally) in 'the original position'; then, from this original position, we are to decide just what kind of society we would like to live in, what kind of a system of justice should prevail. Rawls concludes that if people were thus deprived of any privileged knowledge of advantages and privileges which they would enjoy because of the accidents of birth, etc., they would apply the 'maximin rule',[21] i.e. the rule that under the 'veil of ignorance' one can maximise his advantages by making the choice which would result in a higher minimum-base of advantages than any other choice.

Rawls seems to be proceeding on the supposition that people in the original position would not *gamble* regarding the outcome, e.g. taking the risk on a dictatorial system of justice, on the outside chance that *you* might become the dictator; but, if the consideration that this would be a lifelong choice be taken into account, Rawls is probably correct in assuming that most men (at least those who conceptualised long spans of life in front of them or their favoured descendants) would avoid such risk-taking.[22] At any rate, the net result of the application of this rule, according to Rawls, would be the following pair of principles: (1) certain 'basic liberties' – including the rights of suffrage, free speech on political issues, action according to conscience, holding of private property, and freedom from arbitrary arrest – would have to be guaranteed under the hypothetically just system; and (2) equalisation of social and economic benefits would be attained by structuring society in such a way that inequalities of wealth and advantages would be programmed into a society only where these differences would result in (a) the overall greater advantage of those who were 'worse-off' than others; *and* (b) no suffering to anyone. Thus Rawls' principles stand in apparent contrast to the common utilitarian approach, which is concerned only with producing the maximum *average* welfare for the greatest number of people (whether those people happen to be best off, worst off, etc.).

Consistent with his stringently worked out set of rules for assuring justice, Rawls goes on to note that it is the function of the legislator to give the attainment of justice priority over satisfaction of constituents' demands. A natural objection to this is that it would be a Herculean task for the legislator to juggle all the requisite variables in applying these two principles. And even more basic objections are raised to Rawls' principles: Opponents from the left such as Brian Barry, C. B. Macpherson, and Kai Nielson see Rawls as too embedded in bourgeois, liberal, capitalist presuppositions[23]; opponents from the middle argue that, after ages of inequality, what we need now is not 'reverse inequality', but equality for *everyone* (those best off, those worst off, and those in a middling position); opponents from the right argue that such a misplaced pity for the worse-off would endanger the preservation of cultural and ethical values which are the bedrock of civilisation.

From the conservative camp, Robert Nozick has argued at length and with the greatest vigour against Rawls' principles of justice.[24] Nozick starts from the quasi-Lockean position of 'entitlement', which emphasises the individual's rights to possess all lawfully acquired property and engage in property transactions without undue interference from others. But Nozick, carrying the emphasis on private-property rights much further than Locke, insists that the only function of the state is to protect what its citizens have 'entitled themselves' to. The state as thus conceived is a 'night watchman' state, which functions only as a guard of property, and is *never* to be concerned with such altruistic and supererogatory missions as taxing the better-off in order to provide welfare or social security benefits to the worse-off (just as the night watchman who engaged in 'good neighbour' activities while on duty would have to relax the vigilance for which he is paid, so also the state which tries to function as 'Robin Hood' by taking from the rich to benefit the poor, will necessarily become lax in its essential guarding–policing function). Although Nozick's position seems (to most liberals) quite extreme, he should be credited with bringing to a head a problem in all 'social contract' theories, and first explicated by Rousseau[25]: namely, that if sovereignty really resides in the people, strictly speaking *no* 'sovereign state' can be justified, since sovereignty is inalienable and cannot be 'delegated' to even the most minimal state apparatus. Anarchists of all stripes, from Godwin and Tolstoi to Marx and, more recently, Sartre,[26] have with ruthless logic argued that the only way to establish and guarantee the sovereignty of individuals is to abolish the state (peaceably or forceably, peremptorily or gradually). Nozick, who is attracted by this logic, is more sanguine about the possibility of maintaining *some* state apparatus without compromising individual freedom – and the 'night watchman' state is the result.

Both Rawls and Nozick try to function as mediators – Rawls mediating between pseudo-utilitarian liberals and egoistic conservatives, and Nozick mediating between well-meaning mediator–compromisers like Rawls and extreme anarchists who want to 'throw out the baby with the bathwater'. But in the estimation of Ronald Dworkin, both these 'mediators' are, in reality, representatives of two extremes which stand in drastic need of mediation. In his book on legal theory, *Taking Rights Seriously*,[27] Dworkin focuses primarily on some problems concerning the possibility of making any kind of a contract (even the hypothetical, heuristic, extremely general 'social contract' that Rawls envisions) from the state of such extreme ignorance as is required of the persons existing in Rawls' 'original condition'. But in a BBC interview conducted shortly after the publication of this book[28] Dworkin is more willing to assume, for the purposes of argument, the possibility of such a contract, and argues that the Rawlsian contract would still not be satisfactory, since (a) the requirement that 'no one should suffer' from the advantages offered by the 'maximin' rule to the worse-off seems unwarranted and unrealistic, and (b) the 'basic liberties' guaranteed by Rawls' 'first principle' are only *part* of what people mean by 'liberty'. Dworkin in the same interview then goes on to contrast Rawls, the egalitarian, with Nozick, the libertarian, and calls attention to some basic weaknesses in Nozick's position – (1) Nozick's intuitionism, which presumes that the principle of the inviolability of private property is intuitively obvious to all sensible men, and (2) Nozick's all-or-nothing approach, which insists on potentiating the rather incontrovertible insight that some interference with individual rights is wrong into the rather shaky extreme conclusion that all interference with individual rights is impermissible. Dworkin then returns to the fundamental thesis elaborated in *Taking Rights Seriously* – that *both* the various aspects of economic equality that Rawls tries to salvage *and* the various specific liberties that Nozick champions flow from a single and insufficiently recognised source, namely the basic conception in liberal democracy that each individual is to be treated equally and with due regard to his actual personal preferences.[29] Dworkin's attempts to discover a single primal or pivotal source for rights may be taken as an example of a very important movement towards synthesising (if possible) the divergent polarities of equality vs. liberty, welfare vs. individual rights, that has come to a head in the Rawls–Nozick debate. And it is to an examination of this movement, and the possibilities of this sort of synthesis that we now turn.

TOWARDS A SYNTHESIS

It seems that the final position a political philosopher takes with regard to liberty and equality is heavily influenced by (1) that philosopher's *conception* of human nature, and (2) his *evaluation* of human nature as thus conceived. For example, Hobbes conceived man as essentially egoistic, and saw this egoism as a negative value because of the danger to community security which it posed, and therefore prescribed a strong, monarchical 'leviathan' as the most suitable form of government. Nozick, on the other hand, conceives man as essentially egoistic but portrays this as a positive value (looking after one's own interests, seeking individual fulfilment) on the supposition that the furtherance of individuality is the goal of all social structures, and thus ends up prescribing a form of government which would appear to Hobbes as excessively weak. Some further examples: Rousseau conceives of man as essentially good and altruistic, but also seems to consider this altruism a negative value *in the context of most modern social structures* (which tend to exploit the native altruism of citizens), and thus comes to the conclusion that modern man would have to have very special conditions indeed to maintain his natural goodness at an optimum level (Rousseau's prescription is thus a very small city-state, ruled more by consensus than by calculation of votes, and bereft of any serious factionalism). Marx, on the other hand, although he also conceives man as essentially social and altruistic, saw this basic altruism as a force which had been suppressed by capitalistic social structures and now, with the evolution/revolution of capitalism into socialism, would be unleashed to bring about a total positive restructuring of human relationships. To proceed further: some political philosophers have conceived man as a mixture of egoism *and* altruism. Locke, for example, portrays man as a being endowed with a sense of the natural law and 'conscience' from the beginning, but also recognises that there are corrupt and degenerate men; he accepts this *mixture* as a kind of natural equilibrium, and is optimistic about creating a political state based on this equilibrium (a state which will offer *both* maximum security against the recalcitrant *and* maximum liberty to fulfil one's nature, a political philosophy which will provide *both* strong restrictions against peremptory revolution *and* a clear warrant to overthrow a government if and when it becomes repressive). But Mill, who also saw man as a mixture, was unable to accept this mixture and found it an embarrassment, and thus vacillates between an extreme libertarianism that opposes welfare 'handouts' and favours giving multiple votes to the more talented, more prestigious citizens, and, at least in the latter period of his life, a nascent socialism which would defuse the inequalities between the ascendant middle-class and the still-exploited working classes. Finally, Jean-Paul Sartre, who did not believe there was any such thing as 'human nature', nevertheless in his writings exemplified a constant ambivalence regarding the egoism or altruism of man in the questions he raises (can we really go out in love to persons without exploiting them, can we ever relate to another person as subject-to-subject rather than subject-to-object?), and his vacillation between an individualistic political philosophy and recurrent defences of Marxism seems to be attributable to this ambivalence.

I do not claim that these varying conceptions of, and evaluations of, human nature can give us a sure index to political philosophies in all cases, but only that they may supply us with a useful interpretative device for understanding some of the larger and clearer-cut divergencies among some modern political philosophies.

But if our ideas and attitudes, explicit or implicit, about human nature *are* of some importance for the development of a viable political philosophy and perhaps for an overcoming of the perennial clashes between libertarianism and egalitarianism, the obvious questions suggest themselves: (1) how *are* we to conceive of human nature? and (2) how *should* we react to this conception?

(1) I would suggest that we conceive of human nature not only as a 'mixture' of egoism and altruism (as Locke and Mill have done, and, more recently, writers such as Durkheim and Lipman and Fromm), but rather – to continue the implicit chemical metaphor – as a 'compound' of egoism and altruism, i.e. a sort of union in which conflict and disparity are, or can eventually be, overcome.

(2) I would suggest that we not only accept, or resign ourselves to, the coexistence and possible compatibility of egoism and altruism, but see egoism and altruism as essentially inseparable and fundamentally complementary. Let me explain: true altruism requires a maximum of individual initiative and creativity, personal interest and personal satisfaction; and we can conceive of others' needs and welfare only on analogy with our own, and learn to provide for them efficiently and resourcefully only in providing for ourselves. The selfless altruist who dedicates himself to the well-being of others, if he is truly selfless, will be inefficient, or impersonal in regard to others, and even dangerous or fatal (to the egoists who don't agree with him: the altruism of even the most dedicated altruist does not characteristically seem to extend to the egoists, or those he portrays as 'egoists'). Likewise, true egoism, if pursued in isolation from altruistic values, leads to the creation of prodigies of eccentricity – the Hitlers, the Stalins, the Idi Amins – whose extreme self-seeking and self-aggrandisement (given an altruistic label, if that furthers their egoistic objectives), leads in the end to virtual social and even physical and geographical isolation, and, sadly enough, to the very antithesis of personal satisfaction.

A double paradox may help to cap off the above line of argumentation: The truly effective altruist would optimally have to have the sort of self-interest and self-knowledge that commonly goes by the name of 'egoism' (thus, in Christian cultures, the maxim is to 'love your neighbour as *yourself*'). And the greatest conceivable egoistic satisfaction happens to be in the furthest possible extensions of personal benevolence (again, in Christian cultures, this is the idea that 'it is better to give than to receive').

Of course, this is all very theoretical. In our present socio-cultural milieux, the egoism that we are concerned with is that other egoism that is antithetical to altruism; and the liberty we are concerned with seems to be, no matter how much we would wish it otherwise, antithetical to the claims of equality. Is it possible that these antitheses might be constantly and effectively transcended in *any* kind of a milieu? The kind of milieu that at once suggests itself is one of extraordinary communality, an atmosphere of fraternity in which the interests of the individual and the interest of his fellows are so tied together that neither he nor they wish to distinguish or separate these interests. Thus perhaps it is not just an accident that the French revolutionists, beset with the problem of creating a new political order which would be keynoted by both liberty and equality, looked to *fraternity*, or a newly-found spirit of fraternity, for a solution. It will be perhaps also worth our while to take a look, in Chapter 4, at 'fraternity' as a political value – a value that one certainly hears much less about these days than the constantly warring but possibly kindred values of liberty and equality.

NOTES

1. See Cohen, *Democracy* (Athens: University of Georgia Press, 1971) p. 273: 'Of the three [liberty, fraternity, equality], it is liberty that is the dearest, whose absence is most painful, whose limitation is most quickly noted.'
2. Charles Sherover sums up a recurring theme in political philosophy, in his anthology, *The Development of the Democratic Idea* (NY: Mentor, 1974), in his postscript: 'How much equality can we have without endangering liberty and stifling progress? At what point do the limitations of liberty demand the enforcement of some kind of equality?'
3. Op. cit., p. 15.
4. Carl Friedrich, *Man and His Government*, pp. 298–9.
5. See *On Revolution* (NY: Viking, 1965) *passim*.
6. Note the negative emphasis on 'the absence of obstacles' in this formulation. John Plamenatz, in 'Some American Images of Democracy' in *The Great Ideas Today, 1968* (Chicago: Encyclopedia Britannica, 1968), observes that this negative construal of liberty, found also in contemporary books by Dahl and others, says only the barest minimum about liberty, and must be supplemented with specific positive prescriptions regarding rights of free speech, free association, upward mobility and suffrage.
7. *Capitalism and Freedom* (University of Chicago Press, 1962) p. 195.
8. See Carritt's article, 'Liberty and Equality', in Quinton's *Political Philosophy*, p. 139.
9. *The Second Discourse* (NY: St. Martin's Press, 1964) pp. 140, 156 & *passim*.
10. Herbert Aptheker, *The Nature of Democracy, Freedom and Revolution* (NY: International, 1967) pp. 7, 11, 14.
11. See e.g. Hegel's *Encyclopedia*, § 549, and *Philosophy of History* (Sibree tr.) pp. 18–19.
12. *Philosophy of Right*, §§ 41ff.

13. On the counterproductive effects of simple solutions in revolutionary theory, see H. Kainz, *The Unbinding of Prometheus: Towards Philosophy of Revolution* (L. I., NY: Libra, 1976) ch. IV.
14. 'Even if nature really affected, in the distribution of her gifts, that partiality which is imputed to her, what advantage would the greatest of her favourites derive from it, to the detriment of others, in a state [of nature] that admits of hardly any kind of relation between them.' Rousseau, *On the Origin of Inequality*, First Part.
15. John Rawl, *A Theory of Justice* (Cambridge, Mass.: Harvard University Press, 1971).
16. Ibid., p. 187ff. Rawl's dismissal of utilitarianism may be overly abrupt. Timothy Roche argues that Rawl's theory is not incompatible with utilitarianism, since it is a secondary but indispensible principle of utilitarianism (indispensible, because it offers the security and the moral justification which is necessary to assure happiness). See Roche's 'Utilitarianism versus Rawls: Defending Teleological Moral Theory', in *Social Theory and Practice,* VIII, 2, Summer, 1982.
17. See ibid., p. 124.
18. See Descartes' *Discourse on Method*, Part II.
19. See Husserl's *Ideas*, §§ 18, 31. Relevant comparisons of Rawls with Kant have been made (see, e.g. William Galston, 'Moral Personality and Liberal Theory', *Political Theory* X, 4, Nov. 1982, p. 492), and one might argue that Rawl's 'Maximin Rule' gives final specification to Rousseau's 'General Will'. Suffice it to say that Rawl's reasoning is squarely in accord with a certain approach to the pursuit of certainty, beginning with Descartes.
20. See *A Theory of Justice*, pp. 136ff.
21. *Maximum minimorum.*
22. Or perhaps it would be more accurate to say that they would prefer a 'safe bet' (with low odds) to a 'long shot'.
23. See Arthur Di Quattro, 'Rawls and Left Criticism', *Political Theory*, XI, 1, Feb. 1983.
24. *Anarchy, State, and Utopia* (NY: Basic Books, 1974).
25. See *The Social Contract*, II, 1.
26. See 'Sartre at Seventy: an interview', *New York Review of Books*, 7 August 1975, pp. 10–17, 14.
27. Dworkin, *Taking Rights Seriously* (Cambridge Mass.: Harvard University Press, 1977).
28. See 'Philosophy and Politics' in *Men of Ideas*, by Bryan Magee (NY: Viking, 1979).
29. See *Taking Rights Seriously*, chs 12 and 13.

4 Fraternity? – an Inquiry

> So long as several men joined together consider themselves a single body . . . the common good makes itself so manifestly evident that only common sense is needed to discern it. . . . When we see among the happiest people in the world bands of peasants regulating the affairs of state under an oak tree, and always acting wisely, can we help feeling a certain contempt for the refinements of other nations, which employ so much skill and mystery to make themselves at once illustrious and wretched?
>
> A state thus governed needs very few laws. . . . The first man to propose such a law is only giving voice to what everyone already feels.
>
> Rousseau, *The Social Contract*

> [In the mid-twentieth-century] the term, 'democracy,' was simply a smoke-screen to conceal the real conflict between the ideals of Liberty and Equality. The only genuine reconciliation between these conflicting ideals was to be found in the mediating ideal of Fraternity.
>
> Arnold Toynbee, *A Study of History*

The first recorded use of the triadic democratic formula 'liberté, égalité, fraternité' was in a 1793 motion passed by the Friars Club in Paris. But the phrase was no doubt in vogue before that time, dating from some obscure Enlightenment origin. The obscurity of this origin seems to accentuate the looseness of the connection of these three ideas among themselves – a looseness that would not befit some of the more tightly structured political ideologies, but seems to go well with democracy. However, in spite of their lack of necessary or eternal connectedness, the three ideas do seem to go together: they are indeed complementary, without being synonymous or repetitive or tautologous.

It has often been remarked that America's system of democracy is Lockean in propensity, i.e. with an emphasis on individual liberty as the primary value.[1] Garry Wills, in his *Inventing America: Jefferson's Declaration of Independence*,[2] would like to exonerate Jefferson and many of his contemporaries from responsibility for this Lockean emphasis. According to Wills, while the influence of Locke's epistemological treatise, the *Essay on Human Understanding*, was rife in Jefferson's time, the influence of Locke's political writings was relatively insignificant.[3] Indeed, if we are to believe Wills, it was not Locke but the Scottish philosopher Francis Hutcheson who exerted the most signal and explicit influence on early American political thinking. Wills is not very effective in demonstrating any *general* primacy of the influence of Hutcheson rather than Locke, and in fact leaves his reader with the impression that the undoubted modern influence of Lockean political ideas is historically inexplicable. But Wills compensates for his ineffectiveness in this endeavour by his singular effectiveness in showing the influence of Hutcheson on the thought of Thomas Jefferson himself. And one who follows the logic of this influence can't help but wonder just how different American democracy might be if the Jeffersonian–Hutchesonian influence had prevailed more than it did.

It would not be arbitrary or factitious to label the peculiar Hutchesonian foundation for democracy as 'fraternity', or 'unanimity'. According to Hutcheson, democratic political relations emerge naturally out of certain primal social affinities. Hutcheson, in the style of much of the social philosophy/science of the time, uses Newtonian physics as the analogue for his thinking: just as the attraction of physical bodies is directly proportional to mass and inversely proportional to distance, so also the attraction of social masses is directly proportional to their greatness and complexity and inversely proportional to their natural separation through distance and other factors; just as the internal 'cohesiveness' of physical bodies endows them with greater power in repelling counter-forces from external bodies, so also the greater natural cohesiveness of social bodies endows them with greater fortitude and determination in repelling threats from foreigners; and just as the existence of strong natural cohesiveness in physical bodies minimises the need for artificial bands or bonds for holding their various parts together, so also the existence and maintenance of strong natural ties of affection among individuals and groups minimises the need for strong political structures to hold people together.[4] Jefferson applied this theory in many explicit ways during his career. The best-known application was in the penultimate paragraph of his draft of the Declaration of Independence (a paragraph largely deleted from the final version of the Declaration by the Continental Congress), in which he emphasised that the primary cause of the American Revolution was not the oppression of the British king or legislature, but the diminution of the previously strong bonds of affection with the 'British brethren'.[5] In accord with the same Hutchesonian approach, Jefferson also hypothesised that the American Indians had lesser need for political organisation, and were extraordinarily courageous in fending off foreign threats, because of their natural familial and tribal cohesiveness; and that the overly abrupt immigration of the state of Virginia by those who had no natural ties there would threaten the political stability of the state, and should thus be severely restricted.[6] Jefferson also propounded a remarkable theory of general Negro emancipation, which was geared to avoiding the dire consequences of individual Negroes being set free in a hostile environment with little or no social support, by a plan for gradual emancipation of all Negroes as a *society*, along with eventual provision of territory for establishing a separate but equal Negro nation.[7]

As Wills points out, one of Jefferson's great personality flaws was that he was singularly inept in putting into practice his far-ranging and sometimes insightful theories. But Jefferson did make some efforts in the direction of social engineering – trying to strengthen natural, communal ties to give the necessary strength to the democratic superstructures as he conceived them.

If Jefferson and kindred thinkers had been more successful, perhaps the anthropologist Robert Brain would not have to sum up the characteristics of affectional bonds in contemporary democracy in the following way:

> Democracy involves the attenuation of individual friendships, despite the claim that in socialist democracies we are all brothers or friends. . . . The bonds of affection which we have theoretically extended to the whole society in the name of democracy mean in fact that citizens, instead of making friendships – lopsided, equal, or any other kind – become indifferent strangers to one another, each selling his labour or goods, individually, on an impersonal market. . . . Our democracy does not require strong interpersonal bonds between equals since our cult of the free individual allows members of the community to sever themselves from the mass of their fellow men, even close neighbors and members of their families.[8]

As if to obviate the emergence or counteract the perdurance of such an extreme individualist social desert, some recent voices have been raised emphasising or re-emphasising the importance of fraternity or community to the health and stability of a democracy. Cohen in his book on democracy devotes a chapter to fraternity and concludes emphatically that 'fraternity is the consciousness of community, the recognition by the members of their fundamental, common enterprise. Democracy's need for it is on the deepest level of all, because it provides the context within which equality can be established and freedom can be protected'.[9] Jane Mansbridge in a discussion of just this point reports on the studies she has completed on direct democracies, both past and present, and sees the element of natural bonds of solidarity and friendship as indispensable for their functioning. In direct democracies – from city-states and town meetings to collectives and food co-ops – there is such an intense sense of common interests and friendship that very often there is even no need for voting, and the people seem to look upon their participation more as a friendly get-together than as a meeting. She contrasts this situation with democracy on the larger scale, in which the emphasis is on an adversary relationship and mediation of conflicting interests, and there is greater jealousy about the distribution of power – a jealousy which can only be moderated by the compromise formula, 'one man, one vote'; and she concludes that every democracy should include generous infusions of pockets of fraternity characterised by such direct participation, as an antidote to the impasses and regressions that can result when the 'adversary' concept of democracy is carried to an extreme.[10]

The cult of 'ethnicity' in recent US history is reminiscent of Jefferson's idealistic attempts (discussed earlier in this chapter) to maintain or restore natural and fraternal ties in Virginia and elsewhere. In the early 1970s, Michael Novak inaugurated a new crusade for ethnicity, which he portrayed as 'a barrier against alienation and anomie'. This crusade indicated a laudable recognition of the need for revitalisation of community, but seems to have been no more successful than Jefferson's fitful attempts in that direction. Robert Kaus in an analysis of the miscarriage of Novak's idea concludes that the intensified ethnic identity that it inculcated was not worth the concomitant and entailed sacrifice of the ability of a person to identify with society in a larger sense: 'Although the main goal of ethnic pluralism is to encourage variety in society as a whole, in order to achieve that end it must discourage the cultivation of variety *within* individuals', – which would involve incorporating values of *multiple* ethnic groups.[11] Kaus also remarks that Novak and the ethnicists seem to ignore the obvious fact that most of us would have too mixed a lineage to make ethnic identification even a feasible option. Kevin Phillips, who examines not only the 'return to ethnicity' phenomenon but related phenomena oriented to accentuating 'natural' bonds – regionalism, sex-alignment, black caucuses, etc. – observes that in the context of the great loss of unanimity in America in the wake of multiple economic and political, national and international failures, all such supposedly healthy natural groupings may actually be the presage to the sort of disintegration that Toynbee refers to as accompanying the demise of a civilisation.[12]

Jefferson, Brain, Novak and a small number of kindred spirits aside, 'fraternity' has never been the forte of Anglo-American culture. If we would like to see how 'fraternity' operates in its native habitat, so to speak, we may do best to look to continental Europe for illumination. The German idealist G. W. F. Hegel had developed an 'organic' view of the state as the expression of 'Spirit' – the collective unity of all finite (human) spirits. A sociological counterpart of this theory was expounded in Ferdinand Tonnies' *Gemeinschaft und Gesellschaft* (1887), in which *Gemeinschaft* ('community') as an organic unity was extolled over *Gesellschaft* ('society'). Friedrich Nietzsche (1844–1900), noted as an 'existentialist' antipode to Hegelian idealism, nevertheless developed a concept of 'life' which was curiously similar to the massive collectivity previously adumbrated by Hegel's 'Spirit'. The English philosopher T. H. Green (1836 – 82) propounded a paradoxical possibility of 'spontaneous institutions', inspired after the 'organic' Hegelian model; and another Englishman, Bernard Bosanquet (1848–1923) is noted for his attempts to apply a similar holistic Hegelian vision specifically to democracy as a form of government. In the United States, a somewhat less 'organic' and structured but nevertheless idealistic and holistic view of the state-totality was championed by W. E. Hocking (1873–1966). But the chief, dramatic and concrete consequences of the theory of the state-as-community finally appeared in the fascist movements of the twentieth-century. In Naziism, which drew heavily and surreptitiously on distortions of both Hegelian and Nietzschean concepts, 'community' was thought to be embodied in the race or the 'people' (*Volk*) which was considered superior to the state. Under Italian fascism, which emphasised national pride more than race, the specific differences of fascism from other forms of government were spelled out perhaps more clearly by the philosopher Giovanni Gentile. Gentile saw fascism as the solution to defects in the two major extant forms of government, democracy and communism. For (explains Gentile) fascism with its emphasis on an organic unity-in-diversity avoids both the pseudo-diversity of capitalistic *laissez-faire* in the name of 'liberty', and the pseudo-unity of socialistic class-war and levelling in the name of 'equality'. According to Gentile, the fascist concept of government was unique in combining a natural 'organic' differentiation of peoples and classes with the overarching solidarity and unanimity produced by a massive natural sense of community.

In a way it is regrettable that the most notable modern efforts to work out the political ramifications of fraternity or 'community' were connected with the fascist movement, which is one of the few movements that is consistently loathed now on both sides of the Iron Curtain. For it is at least conceivable that an ethical and non-oppressive government could have evolved with a similar emphasis on 'community'. And it is also quite likely that many theorists, because of their conscious or unconscious connection of the concept of the nation-as-community with the fascist paradigm, will avoid giving attention to a problem which does merit their (and our) serious attention; namely, is it possible by any stratagem or extensions of human ingenuity to inculcate and maintain that spirit of community that we are all familiar with in the context of small, intimate groups, *on a larger scale*, and even ultimately on the scale of the modern nation-state?

Dictatorships and utopias aside, it would seem that one of the closest approximations to the ideal of fraternity or community in a relatively large nation-state in the contemporary world is Israel, a democracy which perhaps more than any other on a similar scale seems to be signalised for a sense of unity and common purpose which is not just explainable in terms of national mobilisation against a common threat, (the sort of mobilisation that gave even a bastion of individualism such as the US a temporary sense of national unity and mission during the two world wars). Palestinian critics of Israel, however, while possibly agreeing that there is an unusual degree of the sense of community among Israelis, would ascribe this political quality to their ethnic–religious homogeneity coupled with a determination to exclude (beginning with the 1952 Israeli Nationality Law) potentially divisive (non-Jewish) elements from effective participation in government, and in the light of these considerations tend to portray Israel as 'fascist' – an extraordinarily ironic allegation when directed at third-generation refugees from Naziism. Although their comparison of Israeli democracy with fascism seems extreme, it should be acknowledged that *any* system of national solidarity based primarily on racial or religious or ethnic identity runs the risk at some point (perhaps in a time of economic or political crisis, as in the case of Naziism) of verging into the intensified national exclusivism that we have come to associate with fascism.[13] And thus it would seem unwise to construct any nation-state dedicated to 'fraternity' (if such be possible) on the provincialism of race or religion or ethnic origins.

At a time when a common belief in the fatherhood of God no longer nourishes a sense of universal brotherhood among God's reputed children, and the Freudian feelings of totemic brotherhood caused by the revolutionary subversion of dictatorial patriarchs is but a distant memory in most large modern democracies, and Marshall McLuhan's famous pop-prophecies that the electronic media would make our fragmented and compartmentalised world into a 'global village' do not seem to be materialising – we must possibly look to nontraditional sources for the revitalisation of community. Some of the most recent prescriptions for fraternity by political philosophers have been gravitating again to T. H. Green's concept (referred to above) of 'spontaneous institutions' – i.e. natural groupings, associations or organisations being given an official, institutionalised participation in governmental processes. For example G. C. Lodge in *The New American Ideology*[14] prescribes as an antidote to the present 'Lockean' fragmentation and conflict in America self-conscious utilisation of existing corporations and labour unions (which already manifest an unconscious evolution towards holism and communitarianism) in strategies for socio-political cooperation. And Roberto Mangabeira Ungar in *Knowledge and Politics*[15] suggests a special adaptation of the European-style 'welfare-corporate state', i.e. a state in which the government assumes a widespread responsibility for the distribution of economic and social advantages, as a solution to the contemporary antagonisms in liberal democracy – a solution which could approach 'institutional spontaneity' via greater government contact with natural social and economic groups rather than via an ascendancy of grass-roots organisations to greater participation in government. It is interesting to note that such solutions amount to a reversion to the 'organic' political philosophy (discussed earlier) of Hegel, who emphasised the necessity for 'corporations' (which in Hegel's terminology comprised labour unions, trade associations, industrial corporations proper, etc.)[16] to act as natural, spontaneous 'mediating' agencies between an atomistic 'grass-roots' citizenry and impersonal governmental bureaucracies. The notion of officially, deliberately planning and providing for a 'place in the sun' for 'spontaneous groupings' of this sort is probably not an example of 'an idea whose time has come' in contemporary politics. For one thing, it becomes more difficult for political leaders to organise a majority out of extremely variegated groupings. On the other hand, the 'art of politics' may at times be expected to require artful probing and auscultation, in order to discern (and even facilitate) a consensus which is not immediately apparent.

NOTES

1. A recent Lockean–Burlamaquian interpretation of American democracy is Morton White's *The Philosophy of the American Revolution* (NY: Oxford, 1978). See also Bernard Bailyn, *The Ideological Origins of the American Revolution* (Cambridge, Mass.: Harvard-Belknap Press, 1967). The classical Lockean interpretation of Jefferson's work on the Declaration is Carl Becker's *Declaration of Independence* (NY: Harcourt, 1922).
2. Garden City (NY: Doubleday, 1978).
3. *The Inventing of America*, chs 11 and 13.
4. Ibid., ch. 21. It is only in the context of this latter analogy that Jefferson's admonitions about avoiding the overextensions of government can be accurately understood. Jefferson did not hold to a 'the best government is the least government' theory in the individualistic, *laissez-faire* sense in which that phrase is currently employed. But, following Hutcheson, he saw the strengthening of natural bonds as the means of avoiding those overextensions of government which would be necessitated by rampant and rootless egoism.
5. Ibid., chs 21, 23.
6. Ibid., ch. 21.
7. Ibid., ch. 22.
8. Robert Brain, *Friends and Lovers* (NY: Basic Books, 1976) pp. 120–1.
9. Carl Cohen, *Democracy* (Athens: University of Georgia Press, 1971).
10. See 'Democracy among Friends', in *The Center Magazine* (The Center for Democratic Institutions) Jan./Feb. 1979.
11. See 'What's Wrong with Roots', in *The Washington Monthly*, March 1979, p. 25.
12. See 'The Balkanization of America', *Harpers*, May 1978. Arguing in a similar vein against the 'new ethnicity', Nathan Glazer advocates a return to the original American 'melting pot' concept. See 'Ethnicity – North, South, West', in *Commentary*, May 1982.
13. As John Armstrong points out in *Nations before Nationalism* (Chapel Hill: University of North Carolina, 1982), ethnicity has a dual aspect: It depends just as much on exclusion of outsiders as it does on feelings of unanimity among those who share the same religious or cultural heritage.

It was such a realisation that led early Zionists, such as Martin Buber, Judah Magnes and A. D. Gordon, to insist that co-existence with Arabs would be essential to the success of their movement. Lawrence Meyer, dismayed that the 'hard-line' Zionism of Herzl, Begin *et al.* has won out, laments that 'Israeli democracy is plagued by a "bunker mentality".' In place of the values shared by the leaders of the prestate and early post-state era – in place of Ben-Gurion's vision of Israel as a 'light unto the nations', one finds increasingly a narrow nationalism, a new tribalism (see 'Into the Breach', *Wilson Quarterly*, New Year 1983, p. 84).

14. G. C. Lodge, *The New American Ideology* (NY: Knopf, 1975).
15. Roberto Mangabeira Ungar, *Knowledge and Politics* (NY: Free Press, 1975).
16. This is also very close to Lockean usage. See Locke's *Second Treatise*, ch. XIII.

5 Majority Rule and the 'Voter's Paradox'

> Such phrases as 'self-government,' do not express the true state of the case. The 'people' who exercise the power are not always the same people with those over whom it is exercised; and the 'self-government' spoken of is not the government of each by himself, but of each by all the rest. The will of the people, moreover, practically means the will of the most numerous or the most active *part* of the people – the majority, or those who succeed in making themselves accepted as the majority; the people, consequently, *may* desire to oppress a part of their number, and precautions are as much needed against this as against any other abuse of power.
>
> 'The tyranny of the majority' is now generally included among the evils against which society requires to be on its guard.
>
> Its means of tyrannizing are not restricted to the acts which it may do by the hands of its political functionaries. Society can and does execute its own mandates; and if it issues wrong mandates instead of right, or any mandates at all in things which it ought not to meddle, it practices a social tyranny more formidable than many kinds of political oppression, since, though not usually upheld by such extreme penalties, it leaves fewer means of escape, penetrating much more deeply into the details of life, and enslaving the soul itself.
>
> John Stuart Mill, *On Liberty*

The notion that the will of the majority *should* prevail in governmental choice of policies and decision-making has been a feature of democracies from the time of ancient Greece to the present. The extent to which it actually *does* prevail in a particular government is perhaps directly proportional to the approximation of that government to the ideal of pure or direct democracy (see Chapter 1). Certainly it is in the very nature of indirect or 'representative' democracy, in which the sovereign majority transfers the actual administration of government to a select group, to take some of the edge off from the full force of majority rule.

For the classical justification of majority rule we must go back to the seventeenth century, to John Locke, who reasons from the fact that individuals through a social contract leave the 'state of nature' to form a political community, that these same individuals should be willing to follow the will of the community, which is obviously expressed by the majority.

> Whosoever out of a state of Nature unite into a Community, must be understood to give up all the power, necessary to the ends for which they unite into society, to the majority of the Community.[1]
>
> When any number of Men have so *consented to make one Community* or Government, they are thereby presently incorporated, and make *one Body Politick*, wherein the Majority have a Right to act and conclude [i.e. obligate] the rest. . . . It is necessary the Body should move that way whither the greater force carries it, which is the *consent of the majority*; or else it is impossible it should act or continue one Body, one Community.[2]

Thomas Jefferson, in his defense of the majority principle, repeats the Lockean argument and emphasises that the ordinary alternative to the will of the majority is *force*, applied by a minority. He tries to formulate an additional justification also in a kind of syllogism:

> Major premise: individuals have basic equal needs and equal rights;
> Minor premise: the earth belongs equally to the individuals living on it;
> Conclusion: the will of the majority is the will that should prevail.[3]

This is not, strictly speaking, a syllogism. If one wanted to formulate Jefferson's argument in a more formally correct manner, he might have to use something like the following 'hypothetical' syllogism:

> Major premise: If no person's rights to the fruits and advantages of the earth shall be weighted more than another person's, then the only way of deciding matters of common concern is through majority rule.
> Minor premise: But no person's rights should be weighted more than any other person's.

Conclusion: Therefore the only way of deciding . . . .

Jefferson, like Madison and Hamilton, recognised the possibility that the majority could get out of hand and tyrannise the minority. But *his* main concern was that the principle of majority rule might not be adopted at all in the actual workings of government, or given only lip service.

Some political theorists have found it less than self-evident that a numerical, mathematical majority of 51 per cent should somehow be taken to represent the collective will of the 'body politick' or the 'people on the earth'. So in view of still-lingering doubts about the classical arguments, less 'forced' and more convincing arguments have been offered by some contemporary political theorists, e.g. Riemer, who appeals to the high probability (in the absence of absolute certitude on any issue) that the majority will know best, and also to the impossibility of determining a 'flawlessly wise' minority (whose will would seem to be the only theoretical and feasible alternative to that of the rather average majority)[4]; and Cohen, who reminds us that it is only in terms of some abstract, 'ideal' state that we would question the validity of majority rule (if we are concerned to benefit the actual people in this or that actual state, then of course it is natural to appeal to the majority actually existing there, regardless of their merits or the intrinsic merits of their ideas, since what is good for them is identical with what they want).[5]

All of the above attempts at argumentation seem in a sense to be superfluous, insofar as they have been made by persons who have already accepted democracy in principle. For one who accepts democracy, acceptance of the majority principle will be automatically implied, although subject to the meaning he attaches to 'democracy'. For the radical egalitarian, majority rule will be a minimum requirement for most governmental processes and policies – near unanimity may be preferred (communist 'peoples' democracies' aiming for such unanimity, often manage to attain 100 per cent voter turnout for their single-party ticket). For the strictly elitist conservative, the attempt will be made to limit 'majority rule' among the people primarily to the process of choosing (élite) governmental representatives. In any government, it is a truism or tautology to say that 'the most powerful' are the ones who rule, since to actually rule is to actually be the most powerful. It just so happens that in certain governments, 'the most powerful' is equated with the greatest *number* – e.g. a strong middle class which is able to mass and organise and mobilise their wealth and energy efficiently towards desired ends. But after power has been equated with numbers in a particular democratic society, the final determining factor as to whether one wholeheartedly accepts, or still has reservations about, majority rule, seems to be his trust in 'the average man' or the lack of such trust; in other words, an attitude or value judgement which is probably not susceptible to any logical 'proof' or justification.

However we go about or try to go about the theoretical justification of majority rule, all sorts of problems emerge when we try to apply it and make it work: should the vote only be alloted to taxpayers, and should the more intelligent taxpayers (intelligence being demonstrated by occupation, educational level, etc.) be given a more strongly weighted vote, as Mill suggests in his *Representative Government*? Intelligence aside, how much impact should apathy be allowed to have on an election? Should the apathetic ones, by not voting, be allowed to relinquish the power of decision on matters of vital interest to small minorities, i.e. to the *de facto* 'majority' of those who turn out at the polls? Or should a quorum be required for a vote to be valid? If it can be shown that the majority of voters were given false information about issues or candidates and had no possible access to true information, should their vote be invalidated? In the case of a 'deadlock solution' (prescribing inactivity in case the votes are divided 50/50), should those who favour governmental *in*activity, and who constitute *less* than a majority, nevertheless be allowed to prevail?[6] If a majority decides on a course of action that a minority considers absolutely immoral (e.g. funding abortions), should this latter minority be nevertheless bound by the majority decision, and can legal sanctions be applied to them for resistance to, or non-compliance with, that course of action?[7] Should individuals who have publicly taken a stand contrary to *democracy* be allowed to vote in democratic elections? What if the majority should decide in favour of, or only elect representatives who will decide in favour of, restricting or abolishing the voting rights and/or other rights of some minority? What if the majority decided *against* the principle of majority rule (would future majorities be limited by this decision, and for how long?)?[8] In the same line of thought, what if it could be shown conclusively that the majority at the inception of a constitution favouring majority rule were actually *opposed* to majority rule?

One of the most interesting challenges to the principle of 'majority rule' is the 'voter's paradox', devised by the mathematician Lewis Carroll (Charles Dodgson), better known as the author of *Alice in*

Wonderland.[9] Carroll offers us a model in which there are three hypothetical individuals (I, II, and III) voting, according to the canons of majority rule, for three hypothetical choices or courses of action (A, B, and C). Let us suppose that the voters, for research purposes, are asked to rank their actual preferences in hierarchical order before they begin voting. Individual I's list is A–B–C; II's list is B–C–A; and III's list is C–A–B. First they are asked to choose between A and B, and, of course I and III choose A, while II chooses B. Then they are asked to choose between B and C, and I and II choose B, while III chooses C. Since the majority preferred A to B and also preferred B to C, one would expect by logical inference that the majority also preferred A to C. But if a separate vote were also taken between A and C, on the basis of the list of preferences already subscribed to, only I would actually prefer A to C, while II and III prefer C to A. But by their votes, II and III (the majority) have already, on the basis of the first two ballots, 'shown' their preference for A over C. Thus the majority are 'bound' by this process to a choice that they did not want to make. Although most voting processes now do not involve the explicit making of such hierarchical lists of preferences,[10] R. Wolff shows that a process similar in its general outlines could vitiate the results of many present-day primaries and elections, depending on the *order* in which various alternatives (or candidates) were presented to the voter.[11] Perhaps the most common way in which something like the 'voter's paradox' takes place in elections nowadays is the multiple-candidate or multiple-party runoffs in which voters, by wasting their vote for a third or fourth party candidate or a 'dark horse', indirectly bring it about that the major candidates who are finally chosen are the least acceptable to them.[12]

While Wolff takes the 'voter's paradox' to be an absolute counterindication of the viability of our present system of majority rule, it should be noted that Dodgson himself had suggested a solution for the paradox, a solution which should not be ignored. Dodgson proposed that the 'voter's paradox' could be avoided if each voter received a certain number of marks to be distributed among the candidates he votes for. In this way, the alternative choices of a voter would be duly weighted, so that they could be still brought into the reckoning if his first choice failed to win. However, as Dodgson also recognised, this solution, 'the method of the marks', might very easily be subverted by human capriciousness: each voter, thinking not in terms of providing for the best compromise candidate in case his favourite lost, and desiring only to maximise the chances that his candidate would win, might decide to give all or almost all of his marks to his preferred candidate. For example, if 10 marks were alloted, then (using our previous symbols), voter I might give all 10 of his marks to A, voter II all his marks to B, and voter III all his marks to C. This would result in a deadlock which would require a run-off or something similar, and we would not have avoided the possibility of a 'voter's paradox'.

The fundamental problem here may be characterised as 'psychological': each voter is afraid of giving any marks to alternative candidates, because in doing so he might jeopardise the chances of his favoured candidate to win. In view of this, Dodgson admitted that his solution would only work if all the voters were public-spirited and consulted among themselves beforehand about compromise candidates.

Glen Allen[13] has suggested a 'modified method of marks' that would prevent such 'psychological' factors from vitiating the electoral process. He suggests that a *maximum* of marks be decided upon to be given by each voter to *each* candidate, instead of some total block of marks to be distributed among all the candidates. In terms of our previous symbolisation, voters I, II, and III might be allocated a maximum of 3 marks to be given to each of the candidates, A, B, and C. Under these conditions, a voter would not have to take away marks from his favourite candidate to give marks to a second choice; and he would *want* to give *some* marks to his second choice to prevent the possibility of a least-liked candidate from being elected. For example, the following allotment might result:

I	II	III
A–3	B–3	C–3
B–2	C–0	A–3
C–0	A–1	B–0

Here voter I gives 2 marks to B to prevent the likelihood that C, the candidate he prefers least, might win. Voter II has a slight preference for A over C as an alternative, but gives A only one mark because he does not want to take too much advantage away from his favourite candidate B. And voter III is interested just in preventing B from becoming elected, so he gives an equal number of marks to C and A. According to Allen, the main thing achieved by this 'modified method of marks" is that it induces voters to consider second choices or compromise candidates and to explicitly include these considerations in the process of voting. This may be true, but Allen's method still does not completely obviate the 'psychological' factors mentioned above: under Allen's system, a voter might still decide not to allot any marks to second and third candidates, for fear that the one or two points he gives them might conceivably be exactly the points they need to attain victory.

Even though it may be possible to find a solution to the Voter's Paradox, it may not be *desirable* to do so. Kenneth J. Arrow of Stanford University, who shared the Nobel Prize in economics in 1972, developed five axioms to defeat the 'voter's paradox' in its various applications (economics and egalitarian ethics, as well as politics), and showed that any system which adopts all five of his axioms ends up in dictatorship. Arrow and others have discovered a variety of procedures which would be consonant with the five axioms, but none of these latter procedures would result in a democratic system.[14]

In any case, it is doubtful that even a democratic solution to the 'voter's paradox' would have any serious implications for the United States and most modern democracies, in which according to minoritarian (also variously termed Madisonian, federalist, polyarchic, élitist) principles there is no 'majority rule' anyway, except insofar as it applies to occasional voting on certain local or state referenda and to the election of certain public officials (in the US 'majority rule' applies to some extent to the election of the president, but it can be, and has been, obstructed by the 'electoral college' system). Obviously, the term, 'majority rule', although it is still used, is a misnomer as applied to any modern government. It would be more exact to say merely that the 'majority principle' applies in congressional or parliamentarian debates and popular elections, counterbalanced and controlled by many other principles. And thus the well-known apprehensions of Madison, Jefferson, J. S. Mill and others about the possibility of a 'tyranny of the majority' have proven to be groundless, although there is always an outside possibility that the majority could under certain conditions exert an influence that would result indirectly in tyranny – e.g. by supporting officials who will implement the desires of the majority to tyrannise certain minorities (as happened in Nazi Germany).

But this is only an 'outside possibility' in a large Western democracy like the United States, in which 'Madisonian democracy' has brought off a compromise between the power of majorities and that of minorities through a 'checks and balances' system. Although the motives for establishing such 'checks and balances' have often seemed to be rather sullied in the beginning (wealthy and upper-class

Americans wanting to insure their rights against possible invasion by the small farmers and artisans who constituted the 'popular majority' at that time, similar to the way that Tories were intent on maintaining traditional class privileges in England), these minoritarian creations have often turned out to benefit poor and disadvantaged minorities as well as wealthy and privileged minorities. Among the minoritarian 'checks' which are established in the US constitution (the Bill of Rights, the equal Senate representation given to small states, the power of states to override a constitutional amendment, the power of the Supreme Court as a final arbiter of legality, etc.), it is the power of the Supreme Court which has perhaps been the most conclusive factor in guaranteeing minority rights, so much so that Justice Felix Frankfurter thought the Supreme Court was turning out to be an antidemocratic institution often effectively countermanding (not just modifying) the wishes of the people by the power of judicial review. Likewise in England ironic states of affairs have not infrequently developed, in which only the conservatives, ideological successors of the Tories, seemed to possess the necessary power or expertise to implement broad and urgently needed social reforms. One might also observe that the legal expulsion of a British MP for refusing to vote his party's line is a paradoxical instance of the attempt to stabilise majoritarian trends through the expertise of an élite (the party leaders).

While the élite minorities have traditionally feared the capriciousness of the majority, and have set up all sorts of 'filtering mechanisms' for majority will, others fear the powers that minorities themselves, privileged and/or underprivileged, have acquired to block normal democratic purposes. Motivated by such fears, Arthur Hadley in *The Empty Polling Booth*[15] suggests in a rather conservative vein that we might be able to get non-voters to vote by allowing postcard registration of voters and declaring a holiday or two in national election years, so that voting days would no longer fall on workdays. A much more radical proposal for restoring majoritarian rule is a plan formulated by Wolff as his own solution to the problems like the 'voter's paradox', and entitled 'Instant Direct Democracy', according to which television sets in every home would be outfitted with instruments for transmitting votes to the legislature every night, after viewers had watched debates on major issues.[16] Wolff solves many of the technical problems likely to be associated with such an innovation, but since he does not work out certain major human problems like 'who would formulate the proposals?'[17] and 'who would take time to listen to the proposals and follow the debates?'[18] or constitutional problems like 'what would happen to the legislative representatives?',[19] there is hardly any likelihood that any such plan would be put into effect on a national basis (although it is not inconceivable that a smaller governmental unit might try something like this with such success that the idea would catch on and mushroom).

Perhaps the most practical proposals offered for broadening the majoritarian base rather quickly in the US are some recent suggestions for changes in the 'electoral college' system of voting for presidents. James Michener, in *Presidential Lottery*,[20] favours what he calls the 'automatic plan', according to which the prevailing 'unit rule' for determining state votes would be maintained, but the function of individual 'electors', who have a potential for causing havoc by voting in contradiction to the expressed wishes of the majority of their state, would be abolished. A more audacious proposal is made by Neal R. Peirce in *The People's President*. Peirce argues for abolition of the unit rule as well as the electoral college in presidential elections and defends his system of 'direct voting' against those critics who assert that such a system would lead to demogoguery, proliferation of splinter political parties, destruction of the delicate balance between large and small states, etc.[21] More recently, a 'Twentieth Century Fund' task force, working for a compromise between electoral college defenders and proponents of direct presidential election recommended retaining the electoral college but awarding 102 additional votes to whichever presidential candidate has the majority of votes – to virtually obviate the possibility that someone with the majority of popular votes might lose because of a contrary electoral college vote. For the presumably rare situation in which no candidate got the majority of electoral votes under this suggested system (called the National Bonus Plan) the task force recommends a run-off election (not conducted by the House of Representatives). Proponents of this compromise claim that it would effectively reduce the confusion caused by third-party candidates (since run-offs would be required much less frequently), and it increases the probability that the winner will have a clear (electoral) majority.[22] It is highly probable that some such reform of the electoral college system will be effected at some time in the future. No doubt, because of the self-perpetuating character of long-standing traditions,[23] the movement towards such a reform will have to be instigated by a crisis or catastrophe – e.g. the outcome of a presidential election in which a president is elected by the electoral college in contradiction to the wishes of the majority of the people (an event that the laws of probability decree is going to happen again someday, and which now, in the days of mass communications and TV, will evoke a degree of outrage which Americans managed to avoid in their more ancient history when similar incidents took place).

But if the movement now going on is successful, it is still not completely clear that the changes that are effected will be for the better. For example, the democratic party initiated changes in the 1972 elections which were geared to assuring that the party nominees would be chosen by the people at large rather than by party specialists. The result has been a more 'populistic' primary competition for both parties. But in 1980 Reagan was elected with only 27 per cent of the voters supporting him, in an election in which only 54 per cent of the voters went to the polls – less than ever before. Considering such trends, one gets the impression that many (including both the experts and the 'man on the street') would prefer to be presented with a choice made by the party specialists who congregate in 'smoke-filled rooms' or conventions. Perhaps a reasonable compromise would be to strengthen the function of the elective élites (the party caucuses, the electoral college, etc.), and then, as a 'trade-off', offer the voting masses on every ballot the choice of 'none of the above' – to throw the selection process back in the lap of the specialists until they come up with a suitable candidate.

NOTES

1. *Second Treatise on Government*, p. 99.
2. Ibid., pp. 95–6. Locke's faith in revolution as a deterrent to governmental oppression made him cavalier about working out the details of democratic machinery. But he did intend that governments established by the majority should be continuously responsive to the will of the majority, as W. Kendall shows in *'John Locke' and the Doctrine of Majority-Rule* (University of Illinois Press, 1959) p. 128 and ch. IX *passim*.
3. Koch, *The Philosophy of Thomas Jefferson*, p. 149.
4. Riemer, *A Revival of Democratic Theory*, pp. 120–2.
5. Cohen, *The Justification of Democracy*, pp. 21–4.
6. Dahl discusses this problem in *A Preface to Democratic Theory*, p. 41.
7. See Roland Garrett, 'Anarchism or Political Democracy: the Case of William Goodwin', in *Social Theory and Practice*, I, Spring 1971, p. 113.
8. Jean Jacques Rousseau saw this as a potential problem in establishing the consensus necessary for a 'common will' in democracy. But his basic optimism about man in 'the state of nature' provided what he thought to be a satisfactory solution: 'In the beginning', or as a precondition for the establishment of any democratic state, there must have been a *unanimous*

consent concerning the (future) use of the 'majority principle' for determining policies and making decisions which would bind the whole populace. Presumably a hypothetical majority vote in a democratic state to do away with majority rule would be self-nullifying.

9. See Wolff, *In Defense of Anarchism*, pp. 59–61, for a discussion of this paradox. The 'voter's paradox' was first formulated by Cordorcet (1743–94), but Lewis Carroll's reformulation is the best known version.
10. But note that in the US many Congressmen and also Common Cause, the 'citizen's lobby', periodically send out lists of issues to constituents (or members) asking them to arrange their preferences hierarchically. A mix up such as the one just illustrated could easily occur in the process of tallying the votes.
11. *In Defense of Anarchism*, pp. 62–7. In the establishment of an agenda for electoral run-offs, an important consideration will be that the candidate who comes up *last* in the schedule will have the odds in his favour. The scheduler can give his candidate the edge by making sure his candidate comes up only after as many as possible contenders have been eliminated.
12. One of the most obvious ways of avoiding this, of course, is by caucusing to reduce the viable choices in number, so that there will be minimal wastage of votes. Unfortunately, there are hardly any mechanisms for, or reasonable fascimilies of, caucusing on the level of popular elections. In view of this, perhaps it is a *salutary* thing that the range of majority rule through direct voting is severely limited. As long as there are more than two candidates to be nominated or elected, there is always the possibility that the very process of voting will result in a choice that the majority definitely does not prefer.
13. See 'Beyond the Voter's Paradox', in *Ethics*, LXXXVIII, October 1977.
14. See 'Rational Collective Choice', by Douglas Blair and Robert Rollack, in *The Scientific American*, CXLIX, 2 August 1983.
15. Arthur Hadley, *The Empty Polling Booth* (New York: Prentice-Hall, 1978).
16. *In Defense of Anarchism*, pp. 34–7.
17. See C. B. Macpherson, *The Life and Times of Liberal Democracy* (Oxford University Press, 1977), p. 95.
18. This is the main concern of Michael Margolis, who is convinced the apathy of the masses would be an insuperable barrier to the implementation of Wolff's plan, and proposes, as an alternative, a massive information network constructed around elitist rather than majoritarian principles. See his *Viable Democracy* (NY: Penguin, 1979).
19. But in all fairness to Wolff it should be observed that those who really believe that the representative's function is simply to faithfully and accurately reflect the opinions of his constituents (as so many now believe) would be led by a ruthless logic to something like Wolff's solution, in an age when advances of electronic communications finally make instant two-way communication possible (see 'Brave New World of Television: Columbus discovers Qubc', *New Times*, July 1978).
20. James Michener, *Presidential Lottery* (NY: Random House, 1969).
21. *The People's President* (NY: Simon & Schuster, 1968) pp. 253ff.
22. William Keech, *Winner Take All: Report of the Twentieth Century Fund*

Task Force on Reform of the Presidential Election Process (NY: Holmes and Meier, 1979). Thomas Cronin, a member of the 'task force', defended the National Bonus Plan as a constitutional amendment – Senate Joint Resolution 123 – in 'Choosing a President', *The Center Magazine*, Sept./Oct. 1978.

23. Although the governors of American states are already elected directly without any intervening electoral agency, this analogy has not and probably will not affect people's thinking about the presidential electoral system. The separation of state and national politics seems to be almost as complete in the mind of most voters as the separation of Church and State in the Constitution.

6 The Two-Party System: Some Qualified Advantages

> But when [a stranger] comes to study the secret propensities which govern the factions of America, he easily perceives that the greater part of them are more or less connected with one or the other of those two great divisions which have always existed in free communities. The deeper we penetrate into the inmost thought of these parties the more do we perceive that the object of the one is to limit, and that of the other to extend, the authority of the people. I do not assert that the ostensible purpose, or even that the secret aim, of American parties is to promote the rule of aristocracy or democracy in the country, but I affirm that aristocratic or democratic passions may easily be detected at the bottom of all parties, and that, although they escape a superficial observation, they are the main point and soul of every faction in the United States.
>
> Alexis de Tocqueville, *Democracy in America*

In Chapter 5, reference was made to the 'voter's paradox', according to which any multiplication of voters' choices beyond two choices can possibly result in a final choice which is not in accord with the actual majority preference. In some countries (e.g., England and the United States), third and fourth party candidates have decried their inability to make significant inroads into an entrenched two-party system. In view of the 'voter's paradox', however, it may be the case that such predominantly two-party systems have a technical–mathematical advantage over democracies with three or more significantly strong parties – provided that we consider it important that the results of final elections should always reflect the actual preferences of the majority of people. On the other hand, it should be noted that even under a two-party system there are frequently a multiplicity of nominees in preliminary runoffs, and splits within the ticket of a single party – so that the 'voters' paradox' could prevail under this system also.

But there are deeper reasons than the 'voter's paradox' favouring a two-party system, at least in certain countries. If there are three or more significantly strong parties in a country, the government in power, often lacking a majority in the legislature or parliament, will have to form a coalition with one or more of the opposing parties, in order to stay in power – a necessity which will often considerably weaken the ability of a government to act decisively and resolutely and without lengthy negotiations with political opponents (unless the multiple parties manage to form a coalition which for all practical purposes is equivalent to a two-party system, e.g. when a stable centre-left coalition and an equally stable centre-right coalition are formed in a four-party system). In a large world power like the United States, such a necessity could conceivably be a devastating weakness in a time of national emergency, when too much hesitation or too long a delay in acting might have irreversible national and international consequences. In the United States, the political system is programmed to prevent any such weakening of the executive branch of government.[1] The President is not *required* to consult with his advisers, and may be able to operate with some efficiency for an extended time without rallying the support of a majority in congress. Such freedom of the executive might not be tolerable, of course, if some maverick *third* party candidate were elected president and had to deal with a congress made up of the two other parties. And so, as if to make sure that nothing like this ever happens, the 'unit-rule' procedure has been applied to the Electoral College in Presidential elections. However, as we saw (Chapter 5), the contention that this electoral procedure, which prevents numerically small votes from counting in most states, is actually necessary for, or even conducive to, the maintenance of the two-party system has been challenged recently by N. Peirce and others.

Another very important reason for the preferability of a two-party system has been advanced by Alexis de Tocqueville, who observes that 'two opinions . . . are as old as the world, and . . . perpetually to be met with, under different forms and various names, in all free communities – the one tending to limit, the other to extend indefinitely, the power of the people'.[2] These 'two opinions' parallel the two contrasting tendencies noted already (Chapter 1) in defining 'democracy'. These viewpoints or 'opinions' seem absolutely necessary for maintaining a balanced and healthy government; on the one hand, the championship of the people's rights, to make sure that government is for the benefit of the governed; and, on the other hand, the limitation of the rights of the majority to insure worthy minority rights and to insure the continued existence of technical and administrative expertise ('élitism' in one of the better senses) where they are needed. In England the Whig–Tory, the Liberal–Conservative and then ultimately the Labour–Conservative, party divisions have traditionally developed along these lines. In the early days of the United States government, the Federalist party had been the party quite unambiguously committed to limiting the power of the people, while the 'Democratic Republican' party was relatively consistent and insistent in trying to extend the power of the people. At the time Tocqueville was writing (the 1830s), the Federalist party had died out and the lack of a clear-cut opposition between an élitist-oriented party and a populist-oriented party was duly lamented by Tocqueville. The opposition has never been quite that clear-cut again. However, it was reinstated to a certain degree with the emergence of the new 'Republican' party in the latter half of the nineteenth-century. During the Civil War era, the viewpoint favouring the 'limitation of the power of the people' seems to have been that of the Democratic (Democratic–Republican) party – with the qualification here that the 'people' upon whom 'limitations' were being placed would include Negro slaves whose liberation was viewed by the opposing Republican party as a potential boon to Northern workers (who had been frustrated in competing economically with Southern slave labour). In more recent times, the party favouring such limitation of power of the people seems to be the Republican party itself – provided that in defining 'people' here we place the emphasis on the average wage-earner with minimum marketable skills, as well as the unemployed and disadvantaged, as opposed to the more resourceful, more highly skilled, better educated, talented, etc. members of society.[3] However, both the early Democrats and the later Republicans apparently learned from the example of the Federalists that excessive adherence to extremely élitist or aristocratic principles in a democratically oriented country like the United States is counterproductive, and the two parties now feature only a slightly different emphasis on many issues.

If we would discern the real conservative–liberal, élitist–populist, polarity in the United States, we would probably do best to look beyond official party labels and stereotypes to the *coalitions* which are put together from members of both parties – coalitions of Southern Democrats with conservative Republicans, of liberal Democrats with Republicans challenging the power of Southern Democrats or Northern Democratic machines, etc. It is such bipartisan coalitions that determine foreign and domestic policies when there is anything like an equitable representation of both parties in Congress.

Whether decisions are made by coalitions or otherwise, they tend to be moderate. In both liberal and conservative political parties there seems to be a tendency to avoid radical extremes. Thus, in summing up the American situation, M. ten Hoor conjectures that, 'if some critic of U.S. democracy will observe closely, he will notice that, if there does happen to be a party which proposes radical change in the form of government, all other political groups sooner or later combine against it'.[4] It is no doubt because of this tendency of the major parties to 'pounce' on radicals or extremists that sapling 'third-party' movements in the US have never fared well, at least if we would judge from the results in terms of the number of candidates elected to office. In a more subtle or moral sense, however, third-party movements may be useful or even necessary for polarising the sluggish 'moderates' (who are the overwhelming majority) from either party. Thus Peter Gay sees the unsuccessful parties in some democratic countries as a necessary 'push from the left', in the direction of the social legislation for which the other major parties get the credit (or blame) when it is passed.[5]

Offhand, it seems that the British polarisation into Conservative and Labour parties is closer to the 'natural' differentiation into élitist and populist wings that Tocqueville discerned. Would it be a boon to democracy if the party polarisation in the US were likewise strictly and officially in terms of liberalism vs. conservatism,[6] such that a person voting for the 'conservative' party could be reasonably sure that his choice of a candidate would be for *laissez-faire* economic policies, fiscal responsibility and the phasing out of federal control over the states, nationalism, moral traditionalism, or a 'hard line' in foreign policy and war strategy, and whatever happened to be the typically 'conservative' positions at the time? while one voting 'liberal' would have the assurance his candidates would favour social welfare legislation, control of wages and prices, taxation favouring the lower-income brackets, etc.? Considered abstractly, this sort of definite polarisation might be best for the country insofar as it would be more conducive to serious intelligent debate on issues than to the nostrums, slogans, and personality contests that seem to predominate in most political campaigns. However, what is good for the goose is not always good for the gander. Such a change to more definite polarisation would only be meaningful in a socio-political milieu where there was a definite emphasis among both people and potential political leaders on constant intellectual debates concerning issues, principles, and ideologies. The emergence of the 'TV debate' in a press-conference format in the 1960 federal election in the US proffered the possibility that intellectual debate might become institutionalised. The subsequent history of the TV debates, however, gives little hope to those who favour such institutionalisation: the number of debates has dwindled from four in 1960, to three in 1976, to a delayed and reluctant single 'sudden death' debate in 1980. On the other hand, a democracy highly oriented towards debate on issues (as e.g. France) is not by any means guaranteed success thereby. Perhaps there is something to be said for emphasis on persons, and the negotiations or deals between persons, as well as for emphasis on issues.

The important thing, the *sine qua non* in a democracy, is that there be some opposition, *some* alternatives, so that the voting public can make meaningful choices. However, we should be wary of professional dialecticians who think that intensification or institutionalisation of such ideological polarisations would *necessarily* contribute to greater freedom of choice. As John Plamenatz, commenting on Down's *An Economic Theory of Democracy*, puts it, 'the two-party system works best where most voters support moderate policies, and the system encourages political moderation'.[7] If one were to draw a graph of the function of political polarisation of democracy, the results would probably be something like this:

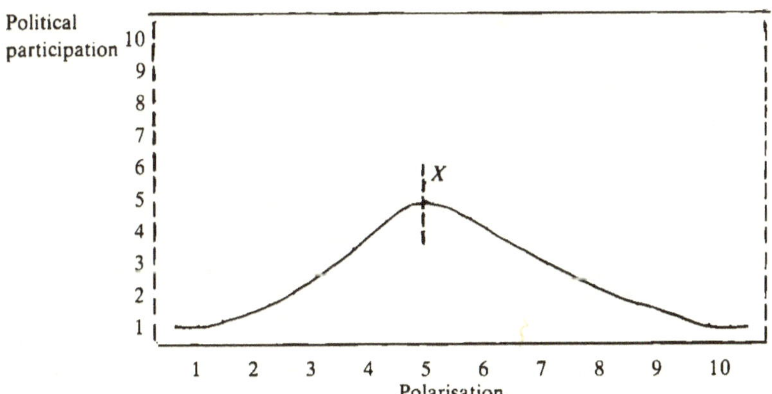

As the polarisation increases to a certain point of intensity (5.0), political participation and enlightened democratic choice is enhanced; but after a certain point (*X*), further increases or clarification of polarities begin to contribute to civil strife and the creation of splinter parties – factors which have the potential of reversing other democratic characteristics such as fraternal unity or majority rule. (A more sophisticated graph, of course, would bring in these and other features of democracy as 'variables', and show their interrelationships with the variable of 'party polarity'; but this is beyond our purpose here.)

In a football game, two sides are chosen and oppose each other on a playing field with predetermined goals; and during the game the sides change positions and play for the opposite goal. In democratic politics, the goals are also predetermined – the good of 'the people' (a phrase susceptible to multiple definitions, as we have seen), on the one hand; and, on the other, the exigencies of 'government' (which, as we have also seen, may mean anything from a bureaucratic administrator of welfare to an impartial referee of free enterprise and individual rights and private property). Within these parameters, it is probably not too important what the two 'teams' call themselves, as long as they are aware of the goals, sufficiently motivated to maintain a constructive opposition, sufficiently flexible to change their goals periodically in the interests of a very high-level 'sport', and, most importantly, take pains continually to make their goals explicit for the voting public. But can such 'sporting' opposition between diverse interpretations of democracy as are found on the national level be equally tolerated and even encouraged on the international level? Some opponents of 'Western' democracy would view this 'sporting' attitude as a typical example of the social superficiality and the merely external facade of freedom to be found in capitalist political systems.

NOTES

1. Some would say, overly programmed. See James W. Ceaser, 'Political Parties and Presidential Ambition' in the *Journal of Politics*, August 1978. Ceaser contends that the present system of electoral primaries begins by putting too much power in the hands of the individual candidate and leads inevitably to 'executive imperialism' in the presidency.
2. *Democracy in America*, p. 88. In G. W. F. Hegel's *Philosophy of Right*, written shortly before Tocqueville's book, there is a similar emphasis on a polarity and dialectical reciprocity of the 'universal' (government and unifying apparatus) with the 'particular' (the people and private interests), but Hegel saw organisations and institutions other than political parties as appropriate instruments for implementing and perpetuating this dialectical reciprocity. More recently Sheldon Wolin's 'The People's Two Bodies', in *Democracy* I, 1 January 1981, uncovers a similar dialectic with specific reference to the American situation: there are two American

'bodies politic', according to Wolin, characterised respectively by (1) a decentralised communal vision (participatory democracy) and (2) the vision of a powerful republic (extolled by Hamilton in the *Federalist*).

3. If, of course, we are thinking of this *latter* group when we speak of 'the people', or 'individuals', then the Republican party becomes the party favouring extension of the power of the people (freedom from excessive governmental restraint).
4. *Freedom Limited*, p. 200.
5. *The Dilemma of Democratic Socialism*, p. 310.
6. Curtis Gans makes such a suggestion as a possible means for overcoming voter apathy due to present ideological ambivalence in American political parties. See 'The Politics of Selfishness: the Cause', in *The Washington Monthly*, October 1973.
7. See 'Some American Images of Democracy', *The Great Ideas Today*, 1968 (Chicago: Encyclopedia Brittanica, 1968) p. 272.

7 The Economics of Democracy

CAPITALISM AND DEMOCRACY

> Every system which endeavors, either by extraordinary encouragements to draw towards a particular species of industry a greater share of the capital of the society than what would naturally go to it, or, by extraordinary restraints, force from a particular species of industry some share of the capital which would otherwise be employed in it, is in reality subversive of the great purpose which it means to promote. It retards, instead of accelerating, the progress of the society towards real wealth and greatness; and diminishes, instead of increasing, the real value of the annual produce of its land and labour.
>
> All systems either of preference or of restraint, therefore, being thus completely taken away, the obvious and simple system of natural liberty establishes itself of its own accord. Every man, as long as he does not violate the laws of justice, is left perfectly free to pursue his own interest and capital into competition with those of any other man, or order of men.
>
> Adam Smith, *Wealth of Nations*

What we call 'democracy' in the Anglo-American and European sense, has developed as a matter of fact in a milieu of capitalistic economic structures: but is there any *necessary* relationship between capitalism and democracy? Is the present tie-in between a capitalistic economic backdrop and 'Western democracy' anything more than an accidental fusion and mutual reinforcement of two historically evolving trends, one economic and the other political? And if their combination *is* accidental and thus dispensable, is the combination nevertheless fortunate and salutary, and thus worth mantaining in spite of considerable internal and external obstacles to such maintenance?

The way that we answer this question has wide-ranging implications: If we say that the above-mentioned fusion of trends is *not* accidental, but a necessary one, then it is going to be extraordinarily difficult for nations like India and Nigeria, which are still outside the mainstream of capitalist development, to make Western-style democracy work in their country (or for us to try to export democracy to them). If, on the other hand, we see the fusion as purely contingent, then we have to open up the theoretical possibility that a state with a non-capitalist, planned (even collectivised) economy, with very little of what we call 'free enterprise', might constitute a bona fide democracy *sans* capitalism.

The issue of the relationship between capitalism and democracy can perhaps best be clarified by consideration of two theoretical extremes – on the one hand, an Orwellian *Nineteen Eighty-Four* style totalitarianism with thought-surveillance and control so complete that there is no room left for 'private' activities; on the other, an absolutely Darwinistic dog-eat-dog type of capitalistic competition, with no intervention from the government. Clearly if we accept the premise that democracy denotes a kind of government in which the wishes of the people are consulted, at least in regard to a choice of leaders, and if we may presume that the majority of people would prefer to dispose of themselves and their labour and property as they wish (and will be presented with the possibility of choosing leaders sympathetic to their desires), the former extreme – a complete absence of capitalistic free enterprise – would be incompatible with democracy. On the other hand, if we accept a second and less complex presupposition that the spirit of equality and fraternity are not just empty shibboleths, but express something of the substance of democracy, the latter extreme – pure and untrammelled licence for capitalist competitiveness – would be equally incompatible with democracy. Thus we might modestly conclude that democracy is not only compatible with but requires a *moderate* amount of 'free enterprise' (capitalism in the loosest possible sense), *provided that* the wishes of the people, as interpreted through their representatives, are in favour of continuing a system of free enterprise.

There is a 'catch', of course, in saying 'provided that . . .'. It is at least theoretically, perhaps practically, possible that 'the people' in a democracy, along with their representatives, might wish to waive some of the 'natural' liberties they possess, including the right of free enterprise, in favour of a system of rigid controls, utterly socialistic, perhaps communistic. In such a case, if we could assure ourselves that the people did indeed act with full consciousness, adequate information, and understanding of the possible consequences, would we be unwilling to grant their newly constituted society the title, 'democratic?'

Although it is not too hard to think of situations in which democratically inclined people might have given up, or actually did voluntarily give up their freedoms to accept a great measure of unwanted controls (e.g. during wars and emergencies), it is more difficult to conceive of a democratic people accepting a government embodying rigid control as a *permanent* situation. It is not impossible, however. If the great masses of people in a democracy became hopelessly impoverished, liberty would become of little interest or use to them. Esau was willing, under duress of fatigue and hunger, to sell his birthright to Jacob for a few bowls of pottage, and there is little doubt that most of us in extreme circumstances would do the same. Herbert Aptheker, arguing from a Marxian point of view, makes much of an apparently prophetic statement attributed to the fourth President of the United States, James Madison, to the effect that at sometime in the future, most likely in the 1930s, problems of property distribution would come to a head in the US and possibly force popular democratic rejection of the safeguards on private property.[1] Aptheker sees this as an uncanny foreboding of the demise of capitalism, this demise being properly inaugurated, of course, with the Great Depression. But, although there was some talk of revolution during the Depression and some doubts among experts about the future viability of capitalism, there was never the universal and abject sort of poverty that would make most people willing to accept permanent limitation of freedom, if not dictatorship, in exchange for bread. Is there any sort of real and imminent danger that could bring about such a universal change now or in the near future? A more sympathetic and impartial critic of capitalism, Joseph Schumpeter, discerns a number of factors currently leading to the gradual but inevitable 'decomposition of capitalistic society',[2] chief among which he numbers rampant inflation, which cannot be stopped by any of the orthodox measures prescribed by economists, and which will assure the relative impoverishment of more and more people as democratic capitalism moves into the future.[3]

Two great classical treatises on political economics have affected modern thought on the subject of the relationship of capitalism to social and political realities – Adam Smith's *Wealth of Nations* (1776) and Karl Marx's *Das Kapital* (1867). Smith, who wrote before the term 'capitalism' was in vogue, proposed a theory of what we now call *laissez-*

faire capitalism, which emphasises the importance of a free market in regulating wages and prices and contributing to the general economic well-being of all segments of society. However, at the time his book was published, there was nothing like the ruthless capitalistic entrepreneurship that would flourish in the nineteenth-century, and there is good reason to believe, from the humane and conscientious attitudes expressed by Smith concerning poverty, that he would have discountenanced the characteristic indifference of the entrepreneurs to poverty, or the claims made that the unbridled profit-seeking of the 'captain of industry' would 'filter down' eventually to lift up the standard of living of the masses. Karl Marx, who hypothesised the inevitable metamorphosis of capitalism in its advanced stages into communism, has suffered similar violence at the hand of interpreters such as Lenin and Mao Zedong, who were unwilling to wait for the mature development of capitalism and industry in their countries, which Marx considered preconditions for a communist revolution; and thus in view of the general lack of readiness of their countries for revolution, were motivated to utilise violent methods to a degree that Marx himself probably never had in mind (Marx, in fact, foresaw the possibility of completely nonviolent revolutions where preliminary capitalistic conditions were optimal).

Whether we would prefer in the spirit of Adam Smith to see capitalism as an adjunct to human freedom and the good life, or with Marx to look upon it as an imperfect stage progressing according to the exigencies of dialectical materialism to more perfect politico-economic structures, it is important that we avoid the tendency found even now among those who follow both viewpoints – liberals or libertarians following (or thinking that they are following) in Smith's footsteps, and radicals or socialists following in Marx's – to think of capitalism in 18th or 19th century terms. It has been pointed out before, but needs to be reiterated on occasion, that there is perhaps a difference in kind (rather than just a difference in degree) between industrial capitalism which was just coming to the fore in Smith's time, and flourishing in Marx's era, and the more recent finance or mass production capitalism (e.g. the oil cartels), in which sophisticated devices such as holding companies, trusteeships, etc. have managed to relegate previous modes of capitalist competition to the status of antiquated curiosities and have *restricted* the opportunities for 'free enterprise' to a powerful minority. Ironically, the only sphere in which industrial capitalism in the old style still seems to be flourishing is in the *international* sphere – where rising stars in the Third World (e.g. South Korea, Taiwan,

Mexico and Brazil) have experienced growth rates vastly exceeding the rates of growth of the industrial giants (the United States, Japan, West Germany, Great Britain, etc.). But on the strictly national level, government has discovered that *unless* it intervenes and controls present-day capitalistic practices, there is no chance that anything like fair and equal competition will prevail in the market. And so, in the last several decades we have witnessed some efforts of government to regulate concentrations of economic power, to protect individuals through social welfare legislation, and to set up watchdog agencies overseeing corporate profits and transactions. And in our day, even a conservative economist like Milton Friedman favours the intervention of government in eliminating laws supporting monopolies, abolishing corporate taxes which encourage internal expansion of monopolies,[4] and even in establishing a 'negative income tax' which would assure a 'floor' minimum income for individuals, while being 'graduated' in such a way as still to provide incentives to work.[5] At the least it is evident that a strict *laissez-faire* attitude on the part of government now would stifle effective competition of *small* with *large* businesses and industries. On the other hand – and this is very important in its implications for democracy – the government can only go so far. Too much government intervention would militate not only against constructive capitalistic competition but against basic personal liberty (interpreted in the classical sense as the right of one to do as he pleases as long as he does not infringe on the rights of others). But it is in regard to the question concerning just how much government control is compatible with individual freedom that there is a major parting of the ways between 'conservative' economists, who will supply you with a long list of items from social security to minimum wages from which government should keep its hands off,[6] and the liberals, who will look in a different direction at things like subsidies to the military industrial complex and subsidies to business through oil depletion allowances, tax shelters and loopholes as examples of unwarranted government interference in free competition. The best-known American spokesman for the 'liberal' school now, John Kenneth Galbraith, also makes an observation which may have some implications regarding the *kind* of government intervention that will prove effective in controlling and facilitating competition: he notes that major corporations now, being definitely out of the hands of old-style entrepreneurs, are run largely by the 'technostructure', a group of specialists for whom the 'law of profit maximisation' no longer seems to hold in its rigour, since the individual members of the technostructure seem to be primarily motivated by the need to change and/or be changed by their fellow members, rather than by a desire for profit.[7] If this were true, it would mean that *forms of government intervention which threatened profits alone would no longer be sufficient* deterrents to corporate aggressiveness and monopolistic expansion. All in all, the process of regulating and fostering 'true' capitalistic competition is becoming so complicated, and subject to so many subjective vagaries of value judgements, that it is hard to blame those who look for simple solutions, whether conservative, liberal or socialist in nature.

One thing seems certain amidst these complexities: the cause of freedom is threatened *both* by the power of economic organisations in the 'private' sector and by the intervention of government. And in dealing with this certainty, there is one strategic mistake that should be avoided at all costs: namely, depending on the *government* to bring about an equitable balance between the private and public sectors, industrial competition and the welfare of citizens, etc.[8] For, as Morganthau observes, a government like that of the United States is not just a disinterested umpire trying to come to a fair solution to a dispute, but is itself one of the principle players in the economic game[9] – not that government officials are profiting personally through kickbacks, etc. (although this happens), but government has come to realise that the cycles of business and industry which it affects directly as a business principal or partner, or indirectly through subsidies and controls, affect the functioning of an administration as well as the fortunes of the political party which happens to be in power.[10] Thus if a solution is to be found, it may have to come from initiatives taken by organised private citizens, whether conservative or liberal in socioeconomic leanings, who will often need to wrench power away from both corporations and government (hopefully by peaceful means) to bring about effective solutions (and the effectiveness of the solutions will depend on how much the solutions correspond to the aspirations of the majority of citizens – provided, of course, that the latter are intensely enough interested and have definite aspirations). It is this element of private initiative, after all, that has been the genius not only of capitalism, but also of the successful alliance so far between democracy and capitalism.

COMMUNISM, SOCIALISM AND DEMOCRACY?

> Just as it is not religion that creates man but man who creates religion, so it is not the constitution that creates the people but the people which creates the constitution. . . . Democracy relates to all other forms of the state as their 'Old Testament.' Man does not exist because of the law but rather the law exists for the good of man. Democracy is *human existence*, while in the other political forms man has only *legal* existence. . . . In democracy the constitution, the law, the state, so far as it is political constitution, is itself only a self-determination of the people, and a determinate content of the people. . . . It is evident that all forms of the state have democracy for their truth [i.e. are true only insofar as they approximate to democracy], and for that reason are false to the extent that they are not democracy.
>
> Karl Marx, *Critique of Hegel's Philosophy of Right*

Karl Marx expressed these sentiments while writing a commentary on, and refutation of, G. W. F. Hegel's monarchically-oriented political philosophy, a few years before he coauthored the *Communist Manifesto* with Engels. If Marx were asked, after the publication of the *Communist Manifesto*, 'well then, have you had some second thoughts about your praises of democracy in your commentary on Hegel?' there is little doubt that Marx would have answered in the negative. For Marx considered communism to *be* democracy *par excellence*, a social system in which the vision and the promise of democracy – the return of government by the people – was finally fulfilled. Marx considered all the governments of his own era, including the 'republic' in the US (which he refers to in connection with the above statements on democracy), as mere approximations to the ideal of democracy. They are all deficient, insofar as they perpetuate in one way or another – through a monarchy, or a bureaucracy, or a landed gentry – the arbitrary and artificial separation of the people from the governing agencies, and consequent social 'alienation' both in the people and in their political leaders. The system which Marx was later to call 'communism' amounts to a reversal of this alienation, because it attacks the root cause of this alienation, the institution of private property, on behalf of which and in worship of which systems of privileges and traditions of hostility have been built up in every modern state, causing innumerable divisions, political as well as social.[11]

When we in the Western world hear the title 'democracy' or 'democratic republic' or 'democratic people's republic' applied to countries in the East European socialist bloc, North Africa, or communist Southeast Asia, we tend to accept such designations 'with a grain of salt'. But it is important for us to realise that those who use this designation are deadly serious. They would *not* disagree with us about the preferability of 'democracy' over other forms of government.[12] The source of our mutual disagreement is the question of *how* to implement democracy. The ideological rift on this question has become so great that the result is our tendency to speak in terms of the 'polarities' of 'democracy vs. communism',[13] and *their* converse tendency to talk about 'democracy vs. capitalism', or 'democracy vs. imperialism'.

Marxists are not the only ones who look to socialism as the paradigm for, or archetype of, democracy. A significant contingent of non-communist European and American Socialists have been making the same claim for well over a century. Perhaps the main difference between their version and the orthodox Marxist[14] version are (a) their definite preference for peaceful evolution over violent revolution and (b) their willingness to allow, or even insistence on including, various degrees of "free enterprise" in the context of an overall socialist structure. (a) The preference for peaceful, democratic means of change is perhaps best illustrated by the principled commitment to freedom of Eduard Bernstein, the nineteenth-century German socialist who believed that 'democracy is at the same time means and end. It is the means of the struggle for Socialism and it is the form Socialism will take once it has been realised'.[15] This conviction was often the source of personal frustration for Bernstein and his fellow socialist 'revisionists', who at times saw opportunities for seizing power by force, but feared that coming into power by force would lead to the necessity of maintaining power through force. (b) Socialist willingness to accommodate 'free enterprise' as much as possible is exemplified in an anomalous attempt to present a feasable detailed plan for 'socialising America', Michael Harrington's *Socialism*.[16] Harrington in this book argues with restraint and moderation for just those few minimal socialist objectives that he considers practically realisable and essential to political progress: the 'socialisation of investments' in public housing, transportation, etc.; the socialisation only of the means of corporate production (not corporate properties), by the use of wage and price controls, gradual acquisition of stocks by the public at large (after the model of the TVA), and other practical measures; and wholesale tax reform which would allow consideration for investment risks, ambition, and hard work, but would penalise passive gains (e.g. through inheritance[17]) and idleness in general.

Thus we encounter multiple and highly divergent social programmes or systems, all vying for the distinction of being called 'democracy'. In order to compare and evaluate these different contenders, it might be useful at this point to return to the Freudian model mentioned earlier in this book (p. 13). Norman Brown, in *Love's Body*, expatiates on this model with specific reference to divergent tendencies in political systems: starting from the basic idea that there must be some kind of killing of, or revolt against, a father-figure (the 'primal crime') to establish the sense of identity and mutual equality (and the collective guilt) of the 'brotherhood' which remained, there are two general tendencies which will then become revealed in this brotherhood – (1) the tendency to assert the mutual equality and self-sufficiency of the brotherhood, as opposed to (2) the tendency or temptation to re-establish the father in one form or another, out of unconscious remorse for killing him. The 'primal crime' has had its variations in the history of Western political systems. For instance (says Brown), John Locke, who in his *First Treatise of Civil Government* was a spokesman in his time for equality and brotherhood, opposed (intellectually killed) Fillmer, who in his *Patriarchia* defended the institution of monarchy;[18] and the American, French and Russian revolutions, following the Lockean pattern, have overthrown several national variations on the ancient patriarchy of which Freud spoke. But even after the overthrow, vestiges of the patriarchy sometimes tend to reappear in one form or another. No nation, for instance, has tried more systematically than the Soviet Union to destroy all remnants and reminders of previous class structures and patriarchal authority. Rights to private property were abolished, attempts were made (during Stalin's regime) to replace marriage with temporary cohabitation and family life with state child care agencies, and the state has been 'replaced' by a central committee of 'workers' and local soviets – but all in vain. The bourgeois institution of the family could not be obliterated, all kinds of compromises had to be made concerning private property and free enterprise, and, as the Yugoslav communist Milovan Djilas shows in *The New Class*,[19] the Soviet bureaucracy has turned out to be a new oligarchy, a privileged class scarcely less onerous to the people than the Russian Czars prior to the Revolution.

After the 'overthrow of the father' has been completed in a nation, how are we to judge whether the result is and remains a democracy? Surely we would not be willing to call the Soviet Union a democracy?

Or would we? In the last analysis, it may be due to accidents of history that one nation, in overthrowing an *ancien regime*, ends up as a 'democracy', and another ends up as what *we* call a 'fascist' or 'totalitarian' state. Barrington Moore, Jr, in *The Origins of Dictatorship and Democracy*,[20] develops the hypothesis that the end result of a revolution is predictably related to (a) the type of personages carrying out the revolution, and (b) the means which they use. On this basis, he differentiates three types of revolutions resulting in three different types of government: (1) a revolution instigated and implemented by force by the middle class with the help of some upper class allies, resulting in 'democracies' (in England, France, and the US); (2) a revolution spearheaded by the urban bourgeoisie with the assistance of some landlords, and without violence, resulting in fascism (in Nazi Germany and in pre-World War II Japan); and (3) a revolution of peasants against landlords in a country lacking any well-formed middle class, resulting in a communistic 'dictatorship of the proletariat' (in Russia and China). Thus Moore is saying, in effect, that the reason some revolutions ended in democracy is that they happened to possess a strong and well-supported and sufficiently aggressive middle class at the time of the revolution – a matter of luck. However, many countries (e.g. in Europe) have developed apparently democratic forms without revolution, and some contemporary revolutions (e.g. in Africa) would be hard to place in any of Moore's three categories – and so he does not offer us any 'rule of thumb' for determining which modern nations are democratic and which are not.

Schumpeter, as was mentioned in Chapter 1, tried to develop such a 'rule of thumb' which would stick to the bare essentials of prerequisites for a democracy, and thus supply a kind of criterion for democracy applicable to socialist as well as capitalist countries. He characterises the 'bare bones' of democracy as institutionalised competition among politicians for votes and the power of the people to choose between them. It is conceivable that we might strip this definition down even further, and require only 'popular assent', at least some indirect participation in government, and some degree of legitimate political competition. Under these criteria, it is *possible* that a country like the Soviet Union or communist China would qualify as democratic if it could be determined (a) that the majority of people voluntarily and fully supported the government; (b) that the input of the people through local elected 'soviets', etc. did often enough determine the policies and decision-making of the government; and (c) that the single-party political system ritualised some form of debate and competition as a prelude to appointments and/or elections to public offices.[21] But unfortunately we can never *know* whether all these conditions are fulfilled. And this 'epistemological' issue seems to be precisely Schumpeter's reason for requiring *explicit* and constitutionally recognised 'fair competition' among politicians. Without some such competition, the wishes of the people can never be explicit, objective, and public, so that we *know* what they are. If a straw vote concerning popular support is taken under a system where only one party is allowed to rule, we rightfully distrust the 'vote of confidence' given by the majority, precisely because they had no other practical and positive choice (voting *against* the sole party would be voting against the government, and would be tantamount to political nihilism and possibly political and social suicide).

If we apply Schumpeter's definition to contemporary Western European 'socialist' countries, we find that all of them meet his criteria for democracy. Among Marxist socialist countries (Chile under Allende and Czechoslovakia under Dubček were possible temporary exceptions and tragic cases), his criteria would not be met, of course. But, as has already been indicated, it is conceivable that at some time equally powerful contending factions within the single communist party could arise, in such circumstances that popular support, in one way or another (not by mob reaction and not by formal voting) would effectively (although not overtly and officially) 'choose' the winner from between the contenders. (It is interesting to note that if the labour union, Solidarity, had been successful in its competition for power in Poland, the ironic outcome might have been just the sort of thing Marx had in mind – a democracy controlled by the workers.)

Whether we are using Schumpeter's criteria or more traditional 'tests' in gauging the approximation of Marxist forms to democracy, the major deficiency of Marxism as currently practised seems to be the lack of public, institutionalised channels for *proving* that this or that government is a popular government; but orthodox Marxists would, of course, reply that the communist 'dictatorship of the proletariat' is a paradoxical kind of dictatorship, in which the oppressed working class simply seizes enough control to prevent its being oppressed again, and eventually will bring about such a complete degree of democracy that it will be self-administered – no longer administered by a 'state'.

As socialism advances in Western European countries, the success of the attempts socialists make to maintain democracy along with socialism will depend, no doubt, on the ability of the country to 'compartmentalise' activities – keeping the gradual extensions of public control over private wealth in a completely separate compartment from those odious extensions of *political* control which would, of course, sooner or later lead to totalitarianism. In Schumpeter's opinion it is possible that this can be done.[22] Democracy, he observes, is not essentially connected with some of the socio-economic features we are accustomed to associate with it, such as freedom of investment, freedom of consumer choice, and even freedom of occupational choice.[23] And there is no reason to believe that all the apparatus of democracy – general elections, parties, parliaments, cabinets and prime ministers or the equivalents – may still prove to be the most efficient means for dealing with the political realities of a socialist order.[24] But Schumpeter is not sanguine about what might happen if this apparatus were shelved, and warns that if socialist democratic leaders succumb to the temptation of controlling the electorate in the same rigid way that they manage to control the economy, 'socialist democracy may eventually turn out to be more of a sham than capitalist democracy ever was'.[25]

In all fairness, it should be reiterated here that we are assessing socialist and communist systems from the admittedly one-sided vantage point of modern Western 'liberal' democracy, which places emphasis on structures facilitating individual liberty, and diverges from democracy in its original sense. C. B. Macpherson would like to go further and re-emphasise the fact that many orthodox Marxist and maverick third-world political systems are really closer to democracy in the original sense than we 'Westerners' are.[26] For in the original sense democracy meant the ascendancy of the lower classes (an ascendancy that was perceived as an 'uprising' by the upper classes, but as 'liberation' by those classes themselves). So, at least on an etymological basis, the socialists and communists may have a better claim on the term, 'democracy', than 'liberal' democrats do. But democracy has evolved considerably since the time of the Greeks, and even many 'liberal' democrats who sympathise with Rousseau's contention that economic equality is a prerequisite for political freedom[27] are wondering out loud whether governmental economic control can be kept separate and distant from governmental control of a strictly political nature.

Aristotle long ago observed that there seems to be an intrinsic relationship between modes of property distribution and concomitant forms of government – such that the economic and political aspects of a society are not separable from, and indifferent to, each other except only through purely mental abstraction. If this is true, it is hard to believe that as socialism becomes complete, through nationalisation of industries, changes in income tax structure, larger and larger deployment of taxes for social welfare, and rigidly administered wage and tax controls, a corresponding tightening of political control will not take place.

The nineteenth-century movement which is referred to as 'utopian socialism' – inspired by the writings of Proudhon, Owens and Fourier – was characterised by an orientation to socialism on a small-scale: highly decentralised local socialist communities, free from bureaucratic control. Most of the modern government-sanctioned socialist experiments – with the notable exception of the Israeli Kibbutz movement – tend in the opposite direction, towards highly centralized administration. Perhaps time will show that this ambition for extensiveness as a mistake – at least if the maintenance of democratic structures is to have priority. Like Christians idealistically trying to 'love all men' instead of their immediate neighbours, socialists striving for massive and immediate social justice on a national scale may be overextending themselves and wasting one of the most valuable natural resources, the spontaneity and initiative of individual citizens. However, the problems of overextension are not just germane to socialism. As we have seen, capitalistic democracy is also plagued with bigness, and one may legitimately doubt whether the spontaneity and free participation that we pride ourselves on is not lost in the intricacies of 'representative government' in which, as Michael Oakeshott points out,[28] the representative is often a kind of ventriloquist who puts his own desires into the mouth of his electors.

In the United States, the inroads of socialism are to be seen primarily in a patchwork of *ad hoc* social legislation regarding unemployment compensation, minimum wages, consumer protection, labour union protection, old age pensions, care for the handicapped and disabled, and health care for certain groups of disadvantaged persons. However, the United States ideologically is also the least sympathetic to socialism, as compared to other countries in the 'Western bloc'. The term, 'socialism', still has a generally non-honorific connotation among the American citizenry. The underlying attitude may conceivably be altered in the future by some serious and long-range economic crisis demonstrating the insufficiency of capitalism. But the interesting opposition of Americans to overt socialism may be more ideologically than economically based – a throwback to the nineteenth-century doctrine of 'manifest destiny'. In its twentieth-century application, this doctrine now represents Americans as the chosen people destined to spread the doctrine of liberty (including economic liberty) and to counteract the subtle and diabolical present-day inducements to regimentation (the doctrine encapsulated especially in the *Communist Manifesto* – the archexample of the extremes of centralisation to which socialism may lead).

NOTES

1. See *The Nature of Democracy, Freedom and Revolution* (NY: International, 1969) pp. 43–4.
2. *Capitalism, Socialism and Democracy*, p. xiii.
3. Ibid., pp. 421–4. It does not seem completely fair, however, for a political economist like Schumpeter to compare the statistical inflation of a country like the US to the largely hidden inflation of e.g., the USSR, where a substitute for inflation is standing in longer lines for consumer goods (what *real* difference does it make if the price of a chicken rises from one-hour's to two-hour's wages in the US, or, while remaining the same in the USSR, takes an extra one-hour of waiting time (which *could* be labour time) in order to be purchased?).
4. *Capitalism and Freedom* (University of Chicago Press, 1962) p. 132.
5. Ibid., pp. 191–5.
6. The Conservative political economist, Irving Kristol, in 'The Death of the Socialist Idea' (*Saturday Evening Post*, March 1979) goes so far as to suggest (p. 53) that 'practically all of the truly popular and widespread support for a "welfare state" would be satisfied by a mixture of voluntary and compulsory insurance schemes – old-age insurance, disability insurance, unemployment insurance, medical insurance – that are reasonably (if not perfectly) compatible with a liberal capitalist society.
7. *The New Industrial State* (NY: Signet, 1968) ch. x. In *The Age of Uncertainty* (Boston: Houghton Mifflin, 1977), Galbraith emphasises the fact that power and incessant 'territorial' expansion seem to be prime incentives for the technostructure.
8. By 'government', here, is meant the administrative branch primarily. It is possible that the legislative, especially if it were supplied liberally with members of the 'loyal opposition', could be an effective counterbalance to the power of industrial 'planning systems', as John Kenneth Galbraith points out in *Economics and the Public Purpose* (1974).
9. Hans Morganthau, *Dilemmas of Politics* (University of Chicago Press, 1958) p. 116.
10. Edward Tufte in *Political Control of the Economy* (Princeton University Press, 1978) marshalls an impressive array of statistics from election and non-election years during the past few decades to present strong 'circumstantial evidence' that the stronger incumbent US presidents, by influencing the flow of direct-transfer payments from the Treasury just prior to election, have managed to instigate a general surge of prosperity that would help to carry them back into office.

11. For Marx's discussion of democracy and related problems of private property, see his *Critique of Hegel's Philosophy of Right*, O'Malley-Jolin translation (Cambridge University Press, 1970) pp. 29–31, 141–2. See also my handbook, *Hegel's Philosophy of Right, with Marx's Commentary* (The Hague: Nijhoff, 1974) pp. 56–7, 82–3.
12. As Charles Stevenson points out in *Ethics and Language* (New Haven: Yale University Press, 1944), 'democracy' has retained the same positive connotations under communist governments as it had in the US and other Western governments. And the communists are not the only ones who have taken over the word. As Jack Lively remarks, 'Democracy is . . . a "hurrah" word in the sense that, in the contemporary world, there are few who will take an explicit stand against the legitimacy of democracy. . . . On self-description, Rhodesia, South Africa and Tanzania as well as Russia and America are democracies; even military regimes commonly seek justification by pledging themselves to the ultimate restoration of democracy (usually in the purified form resulting from the elimination of politicians)' (*Democracy*, NY, Capricorn, 1977, p. 2).
13. This is not a universal tendency, however. Some writers of left-of-centre persuasions in America tend to equate democracy with Marxism. See, for example, Megill's *The New Democratic Theory* (NY: Free Press, 1970).
14. There are 'independent' or 'critical' Marxists who are against violent revolution, favour free enterprise, and even advocate religion – positions which are welcomed by 'Western' liberal democrats, but definitely seem to compromise orthodox Marxist principles, so that they cannot really be labelled 'Marxist'; as, for example, Christian theologians who do not believe in the divinity of Jesus or resurrection or immortality are not 'Christian' in any orthodox sense. In this respect, the efforts of Soviet Marxist–Leninists to maintain strict Marxist orthodoxy makes sense. The 'heretics' who wish to amalgamate Marx's insights with principles essential to Western liberal democracy, should perhaps, in the interests of clarity, be designated 'socialists' or at most 'Marxians' rather than 'Marxists'.
15. See Peter Gay, *The Dilemma of Democratic Socialism* (NY: Collier, 1970) p. 303.
16. Michael Harrington, *Socialism* (NY: Bantam, 1973).
17. In his position concerning inheritance taxes, Harrington has received some strong support from a major non-socialist research centre. A report from the Brookings Institution states that the chief cause of inequality of wealth in both the US and Britain is inheritance. Large estates of sons are positively correlated with large estates of fathers. 1% of American families own 25% of all personal wealth, and the lowest 46% of American families own 2% of personal wealth. See John Brittain, *Inheritance and the Inequality of Material Wealth* (Washington, DC: The Brookings Institution, 1979). The author in summing up the thrust of the report points to high inheritance taxes in the upper brackets as the single most important measure that could be taken to achieve more equitable distribution of wealth.
18. *Love's Body* (NY: Vintage, 1966) p. 4.
19. Milovan Djilas, *The New Class* (NY: Praeger, 1957).

20. Barrington Moore, Jr, *The Origins of Dictatorship and Democracy* (Boston: Beacon Press, 1967).
21. C. B. Macpherson, in *The Real World of Democracy* (Oxford University Press, 1975) p. 21, would also add the requirement that membership in such a single-party system be open to all, even citizens who were non-activist.
22. *Capitalism, Socialism and Democracy*, p. 229. Schumpeter's sanguine view of the possibility of a democratic socialism is shared by Charles Lindblom. In his *Politics and Markets: the World's Political-Economic Systems* (NY: Basic Books, 1977), Lindblom divides political structures into (1) authoritarian and (2) polyarchal (democratic); and economic systems into (a) preceptorial, centrally-planned and (b) market-oriented. He notes that although clear-cut cases of type (2) (a) are conspicuously lacking in the world today, there is no compelling reason why such a species of government might not develop and flourish.

    E. F. Schumacher in *Small is Beautiful* (NY: Perennial Library, 1975) pp. 283–4, lists 3 basic options, the first two of which are similar to those in Lindblom's schema: (1) Freedom vs. totalitarianism (F vs. T); (2) Market economy vs. planning (M vs. P); and (3) Private ownership vs. public or collectivised ownership (PO vs. CO). Because of the addition of the third option, he comes out with 8 possible combinations: (1) F+M+PO; (2) F+P+PO; (3) F+M+CO; (4) F+P+CO; (5) T+M+PO; (6) T+P+PO; (7) T+M+CO; (8) T+P+CO. Schumacher adds that, while we tend to think in terms of just combination # 1 and combination # 8, all the intermediary combinations are conceivable.
23. Schumpeter, p. 411.
24. Ibid., p. 301.
25. Ibid., p. 302.
26. *The Real World of Democracy*, pp. 12–13.
27. See *The Social Contract*, II, 111; also III, 13.
28. 'The Masses in Representative Democracy', in *Freedom and Serfdom*, A. Hunold ed., R. Stevens tr. (Dordrecht, Netherlands: D. Reidel, 1961) p. 167.

8 Religion in a Democracy

Much vague and sentimental journalism has been poured out to the effect that Christianity is akin to democracy, and most of it is scarcely strong or clear enough to refute the fact that the two things have often quarrelled. The real ground upon which Christianity and democracy are one is very much deeper.

The mere machinery of voting is not democracy, though at present it is not easy to effect any simpler democratic method. But even the machinery of voting is profoundly Christian in this practical sense – that it is an attempt to get at the opinion of those who would be too modest to offer it. . . . There is something psychologically Christian about the idea of seeking for the opinion of the obscure rather than taking the obvious course of accepting the opinion of the prominent. . . . Canvassing is very Christian in its primary idea. It is encouraging the humble; it is saying to the modest man, 'Friend, go up higher . . .'.

Aristocracy is not an institution: aristocracy is a sin; generally a very venial one. It is merely the drift or slide of men into a sort of natural pomposity and praise of the powerful, which is the most easy and obvious affair in the world. . . .

It is the peculiar honour of Europe since it has been Christian that while it has had aristocracy it has always at the back of its heart treated aristocracy as a weakness – generally as a weakness that must be allowed for. If any one wishes to appreciate this point, let him go outside Christianity into some other philosophical atmosphere. Let him, for instance, compare the classes of Europe with the castes of India. There aristocracy is far more awful, because it is far more intellectual. It is seriously felt that the scale of classes is a scale of spiritual values; that the baker is better than the butcher in an invisible and sacred sense. But no Christianity, not even the most ignorant or perverse, ever suggested that a baronet was better than a butcher in that sacred sense. No Christianity, however ignorant or extravagant, ever suggested that a duke would not be damned. . . . In Christian society we have always thought the gentleman a sort of joke. . . . The English aristocracy is not only the type, but is the crown and flower of all actual aristocracies. . . . The great and very obvious merit of the English aristocracy is that nobody could possibly take it seriously.

G. K. Chesterton, *Orthodoxy*

Arnold Brecht, who poses numerous challenges for political scientists in his *Political Theory*, ends the book questioning the now-accepted tradition among political scientists of 'bracketing' questions about God and religion, setting them to the side as irrelevant, and especially avoiding dependence on religious beliefs as a *source of knowledge* about our political institutions (and not just as a phenomenon in the social realm).[1]

Although conceding that the separation of the interests of political science from religion was necessary at a certain stage, he conjectures that we may have now reached the stage where it would be beneficial to relax taboos, consider the existence of God and religious needs in man to be 'working hypotheses', and patiently try to determine whether these hypotheses are able to throw any light on our political situation(s).

At the very least, the study of religion should be included in political science to the extent that religion expresses, in rational or symbolic form, real inner experiences, which are bound to have an effect on personal activities in the political sphere and even, perhaps, on basic political structures. There is even greater reason for studying religion as a prelude to political thinking if, as the social philosopher Émile Durkheim contended, religious beliefs and rituals seem to be directly related to the governing concepts which a society forms of itself and its environment. Durkheim tried to show, for instance, that the concept of a god in primitive society was an official personification of the clan; that religious beliefs were originally the source of man's notion of classes; and that reverence for the sacred in religion was a symbol of the sentiments a society possessed about its own uniqueness. Claude Lévi-Strauss followed the same general line of thought – that religion expresses basic social realities – and went even further, with a hypothesis that religion is an attempt to lend order and full-scale coherence, in any particular era, to the findings of physical and social science, which are always doomed to imperfection and shortsightedness. Karl Marx, following Feuerbach, treated the idea of God as a projection of unfulfilled possibilities for creativity and productivity in a society, but was not interested in the study of religion *per se*, since he saw this mechanism of projection as alienating, a fundamentally unhealthy phenomenon (which needs to be discouraged, extirpated and transcended, not to be studied). Freud likewise saw religious 'projections' as unhealthy, but worth study in so far as they have a potential for pinpointing pathological tendencies in an individual's relationship to authority figures, including public authorities and the state itself.

None of these thinkers actually takes religion as an authority for determining the nature of political society or the values which ought to imbue the latter. But they all, from strikingly different vantage points, see religious concepts as intimately or necessarily connected with socio-political structures. In a very real sense, for them there is no such thing as a separation of church and state. If there is a *church* or religion, it cannot exist independent from, and indifferent to, political realities. This realisation has led to quite divergent conclusions: for example, in Marx's estimation the eradication or phasing out of religion was necessary for the emergence of an optimal non-alienated, democratic society; while for Durkheim religion was one of the two essential instruments (along with education) for successfully reforming society.

On the other hand, it is quite possible (*contra* Durkheim) that we could start with a reformation of society – and *then* a radical change in religion (whether reform, amelioration, or perhaps extinction à la Marx) would be the consequence. There is a '. . . the chicken or the egg?' type of question here as to which is first. Perhaps the most we could say is that there seems to be some reciprocal relationship between religion and political forms, such that, at least at present, they should be considered as mutually conditioning, although independent, variables.

If this be the case, it is to be expected that we who are interested in the subject of democracy should take the next logical step and ask, 'could there be a kind of universal interrelationship between religious forms and modern political structures, such that democracy might thrive where certain religions prevail, but flounder when other religions or even atheism gain the ascendancy?' Perhaps no one has affirmed the general interrelationship between religion and political forms more firmly than G. W. F. Hegel (1770–1831), who in his (posthumous) *Philosophy of History* states, 'the form of Religion . . . decides that of the State and its constitution'.[2] In Hegel's estimation, it was only under the aegis of the Protestant religion that a fully free state (which he equated with 'constitutional monarchy') could flourish. The reasons he gives for this are somewhat technical: Protestantism is the form of Christianity in which the synthesis has finally been achieved between universality and (subjective) particularity, between consciousness and (individual) self-consciousness.[3] Catholicism, in contrast, in which there is a kind of ever-perpetuated dichotomy between the universal and the particular, is allegedly a hostile environment to the most modern aspirations for self-determination and freedom of conscience.

A more empirically grounded thesis with possible implications for political philosophy is propounded by Max Weber, who contended that a Calvinistic type of Protestantism was causally related to the emergence of capitalism. Weber very artfully draws parallels between the Calvinist sense of a 'calling' and growing bourgeois pride and élitism in the nineteenth-century world; between the anxious search of Calvinists for assurances of 'predestination' (to heaven) and the businessman's pragmatic orientation to concrete signs of success; between Calvinist asceticism, which discouraged pleasure in profits as well as other pleasures, and the distinctively capitalistic penchant for assiduously and religiously saving and repeatedly reinvesting profits made.[4] If what 'Western' nations like the United States like to call 'democracy' is related to capitalist economic structures (see the first section of Chapter 7), then, if Weber is correct, the ideals of Protestantism in the US may be necessary and sufficient conditions for democracy (as some of the more anti-Catholic Founding Fathers used to maintain). However, after the excitement over Weber's thesis crested, critics began to point out that Weber's theory did not seem to be justifiable when applied to specific European and American Calvinist-oriented communities: for example, the capitalist elements which began to infiltrate New England society in the seventeenth-century were not noted for their serious adherence to strict Puritan religious ideals and observances. There seems to be some evidence, on the other hand, that after capitalism began to flourish, there was, as a matter of fact, a convergence or natural affinity between the economic style and *modus operandi* of capitalists and the strict and self-disciplined and results-oriented Calvinist-style Protestantism.

Sacvan Bercovitch, who in *The Puritan Origins of the American Self*[5] resurrects Weber's thesis about the Calvinist–Puritan roots of American national characteristics, nevertheless takes a different tack in trying to establish this: instead of simply focusing on similar values in American life and its religious counterpart, Bercovitch portrays American life as a massive fulfilment of the Puritan religious vision of men like Cotton Mather, to such a degree that the distinction between 'religious' and 'secular' becomes blurred. According to Bercovitch, the

American colonists under Puritan influence began to consider themselves the true Israelites fleeing from Babylon (the Old World) to the New Canaan (America) by means of a kind of mass baptism (the crossing of the ocean), in order to establish God's kingdom on earth, the New Zion. Bercovitch concurs with Weber in tracing the capitalistic virtues of industriousness and thrift to Calvinist origins.

But neither Weber nor Bercovitch establish anything more than a contingent historical connection between Protestantism and American capitalism. They could not supply much grist for the mill of someone who would like to pinpoint some more necessary and permanent connection of democracy and religion.

Weber and Bercovitch have perhaps erred in looking to a specific religious persuasion for causal explanations of social phenomena. Carl J. Friedrich avoids doing this, and offers a somewhat more creditable account of how general perennial religious orientations, beliefs and adjuncts carried over into the secular realm to produce many of the 'constitutional' principles and rituals that we have come to associate with a democratic country like the US.

According to Friedrich, the old ideas about the alliance of rulers with God ('divine right' of kings, etc.) have now been transformed, in democracy, into the idea that the Constitution is sacred; the rituals formerly used to invest kings are retained minimally in what we call the Oath of Office; ancestor worship, such a boon to stability in ancient times, has been supplanted in America by the rituals of the Daughters of the American Revolution and similar public testimonials to eminent Americans of the past; and perhaps most important, our notions of basic inviolable human rights and the dignity of the individual have not been derived from Greece and Rome (in which only certain limited political rights were recognised), but from the evolution of the ideas of justice and divine justice from the beginnings of Christianity through the Middle Ages to the present.[6]

Whether we agree or not with the theses of Weber, Bercovitch or Friedrich, it is a matter of historical fact that religious beliefs were important motivating factors in the minds of men like Thomas Jefferson at the time of the establishment of the American democratic republic, and at least very general religious influences on political developments in America can be traced back to the life and works of Jonathan Edwards, George Whitfield and other important religious figures of the eighteenth century.[7] The knowledge that this is the case leads us to wonder: could a very similar democratic framework have arisen (and/or be maintained at present) – (a) under very different religious auspices?; (b) under very different Christian auspices? and (c) under irreligious or anti-religious auspices (agnosticism or atheism). There is, of course, no way of knowing exactly what would have happened in the socio-political realm under these very different influences, since there are so many and complex variables in human affairs. But if we adhere to very broad parameters, there are certain general but relevant observations that could be made with some degree of self-evidence.

THE VARIETIES OF RELIGION AND DEMOCRACY

The conception of God which prevails in a certain society is bound to have some significant effect on political structures and patterns of socially approved behaviour: (1) a society in which there is a conception of God as severe, exacting, jealous and swift in meting out justice, and which *admires* God for these attributes, is likely to approve or accept the same attributes in their governing official or officials (we might point to the revolutionary Islamic republic in Iran under the Ayatollah Ruhollah Khomeini as a case-in-point); (2) that society, on the other hand, which conceptualises God as mild, easy-going, forgiving – an all-around 'good guy' – is not likely to be oriented to a severe and authoritarian political structure; (3) where God is thought to be 'transcendent' – i.e. separate from and superior to all creation, including creatures who happen to be political leaders – the authority of these latter political leaders could not be consistently considered the 'last word', but should be subject to challenges, either institutionalised or originating from individuals; and (4) where, conversely, God is thought to be 'immanent' in a state, e.g. incarnated in an Emperor who is taken to be the 'son of God', or seen as quasi-incarnate in priest or pope (in a situation where the latter are allied with political authorities), the independent questioning attitude, referred to above, would be unconscionable. If any one of the above notions of God prevailed almost universally in a given society, and was strongly and emotionally *approved* by that society, and if the members of that society did not have some government or way of living enforced on them by foreign or external pressures, then predilections could be predicted to range in the directions indicated. Otherwise, there would be such a wide cleavage between theological and social attitudes that something like wholesale mental disease would result.

With regard to the development of a stable and efficient *democracy*, it would seem that a certain mixture or synthesis of all these diverse concepts of God would be at least useful: (1) a conception of the justice and ultimate firmness of God, as conducive to the formation of habits of personal discipline, hard work, and accountability in the democratic citizenry; (2) the idea of God's concern and mercy, as conducive to attitudes of mutual helpfulness and toleration; (3) the idea of God's transcendence, to emphasise the limitations of secular authority, and to assure a higher court of appeal (one's conscience as the voice of God) beyond political spheres; and (4) the notion of the immanence of God in at least a restricted fashion, to assure civil order and sufficient respect for civil authorities.

The Judaeo-Christian tradition, as a synthesis of the ideas of (1) a stern and just God with (2) a merciful and forgiving God, and of (3) a God who stands outside history but (4) enters into history in a provident manner – would seem to be pre-eminently suited to maintaining an equilibrium of the above-mentioned values in a democratic society. Although elements of these syntheses may be found in all other great world religions, Christianity, the only religion which places primary emphasis on the incarnation of God and on the God-man as a personal, concrete synthesis of immanence, transcendence, etc., may be uniquely qualified as a *symbolic* foundation for democratic structures. This is not to suggest, however, that Christianity should have power of administrative jurisdiction over the state and/or over other religions. In fact, such power or jurisdiction would seem to contradict the basic principles of Christianity, which preaches that religion must give to Caesar the things that are Caesar's, that the first shall be last, and that the ruler shall be the servant of all.

THE VARIETIES OF CHRISTIANITY AND DEMOCRACY

There are three commonly assumed democratic values that seem to be particularly traceable to Christianity, at least ideal Christianity as adumbrated in the Gospels: (1) the idea that the leader should be a 'public servant' rather than a lord and master of his subjects, which is the secular version of Jesus' admonitions (Mark x, 42ff) to his disciples that 'the greatest among you shall be the least', and that the followers of Christ should not lord it over one another 'like the pagans'; (2) the notion that man directed by the Holy Spirit (read 'conscience' in the secularised-political sphere) should be free from external laws, and can never be wholly subservient to 'Caesar' (see Matt. xvii, 34ff, Rom. vii, 1–7); and (3) the insistence on the brotherhood (read 'equality' in the secularised version) of all Christians (see Acts I, 16; Rom. I, 13; I Cor. xv, 58; etc.).

In the Roman Catholic church, although the Pope calls himself 'the servant of the servants of God', there has been until recent times an aristocracy and pomp and a hierarchical organisation that was ill-suited to egalitarianism, humility in the upper echelons, and an atmosphere of religious libertarianism. Insofar as there are still remnants of monarchical–aristocratic structures in Catholicism, one might conclude that Roman Catholicism is less readily supportive of democratic values than most forms of Protestantism, which at least officially de-emphasise or completely disallow any such reminders of 'Romanism'.[8] However, after the General Council (Vatican II) of the 1960s, there has been an extraordinary and accelerating movement towards decentralisation and liberalisation in the Catholic Church that has brought it closer to the 'spirit' of Protestantism – so that, while the two persuasions are still quite distinct, they no longer seem rigidly antithetical.

Irving Kristol in several places[9] suggests that the Protestant spirit (which in Kristol's view is not terribly heterogeneous with the Catholic spirit at present) is an indispensable bulwark of capitalistic democracy against nihilism. Without that sense of direction, moral purpose and inculcation of moral restraint that comes only through this religious spirit, says Kristol, capitalism, blissfully neutral towards whether its profits come from pornography or potatoes, must eventually 'self-destruct' and be buried by socialism.

ATHEISM AND DEMOCRACY

A public, committed, organised and proselytising sort of atheism is rather rare in Western society, as compared with correspondingly dedicated forms of theism. But we may still ask the question, what would be the probable influence of atheism on democracy in a society if atheism became widespread? In order to discern any correspondences here, one must first realise that there are atheisms and – there are atheisms. There is an atheism which makes much of the thesis that man is 'nothing but' a collection of material elements, has only one life to live, and will not be held accountable for his deeds in any 'hereafter'. It is possible that such a negativistic species of atheism could adversely affect democratic suppositions concerning the dignity of the individual,[10] and that one who really *believes* in it would not be likely to be willing to make any extraordinary sacrifices to assure the welfare of future generations or even for the present generation (e.g. risking his life on the battlefield or engaging on a volunteer basis in strenuous and irksome civil duties or civil litigations on behalf of the rights of those with whom he does not agree or sympathise). There is also a more idealistic sort of 'humanistic atheism' (e.g. as embraced by Marx, Nietzsche, Sartre), which sees the 'transcendence' of God as an offense to, and derogation of, man and tries to redirect what were once transcendently-oriented religious impulses towards man himself, and towards ameliorating the human situation. But the commendable interest in man exemplified in such humanistic atheisms is not always conducive to *democratic* ideals: Nietzsche's interest in creative individuality led him to despise 'herd-oriented' democracy; Sartre's emphasis on the absolute freedom of the individual must be qualified, if not compromised, by his temporary espousal of Stalinism and subsequent defence of that position[11] and his rather constant defence of specific terrorist groups;[12] and Marx's concern for the working classes has given rise to the Leninist and Stalinist interpretations (or distortions) of Marxism which seem to be far removed from the basic ideals of democracy. It is worth noting that John Dewey, who rejected traditional religion, felt it necessary to recommend a naturalistic religion, or a transference of 'religious' behaviour from the supernatural to the natural realm, in order to bolster and foster the democratic way of life, with its emphasis on fluidity and openness to change and the 'experimental' approach to government. Thus Dewey, in his unwillingness to do away with religion completely, seems to offer graphic confirmation of Alexis de Tocqueville's fear that,

> when there is no longer any principle of authority in religion any more than in politics, men are speedily frightened at the aspect of this unbounded democratic independence. The constant agitation of all surrounding things alarms and exhausts them. As everything is at sea in the sphere of the mind, they determine at least that the mechanism of society shall be firm and fixed; and as they cannot resume their ancient belief, they assume a master.[13]

Tocqueville's premonition is suggestive insofar as it calls our attention to a possible 'danger' in atheism for democracy – namely, that the feeling of unlimited independence which it engenders may cause a rebound of psychic anxiety, and a desire to re-establish in *society itself* some grounding or authority as 'fixed and inflexible' as the notions of God used to be. If we are interested in maintaining the pliability and openness of democracy intact, perhaps the sort of natural religion suggested by Rousseau, Comte, Dewey or Huxley is called for, to divert man's natural religious impulses from 'transcendental' goals to humanistic and ethical objectives; or perhaps an atheism of the more moderate sort, i.e. formal and articulate agnosticism, may be conducive to liberal democratic tendencies simply because of the absence of ideology and absolutes, the openness of mind, implied in such a position (although agnosticism, like any other stand, could be adhered to as an orthodox ideology and an absolute).

On a purely empirical basis – since the only examples we have of widespread and public commitment to atheism are in the Soviet Union and many other communist nations – we would have to say that atheism does not seem to be always or even most of the time a step toward 'liberal' democracy. And yet, at least in its concept, the humanistic type of atheism, which is committed to the ideals of universal freedom and human welfare here and now, would seem to be eminently suited to the promotion of democratic forms of government – provided that the enthusiasm and dedication to finite man can be maintained at least at the same level of energy formerly inspired by the idea of an infinite[14] God. Such a distinction as we are making here between humanistic atheism (some call it 'positive' atheism) and negativistic atheism is reminiscent, in a way, of Kierkegaard's famous distinction between 'Christianity' (a religion which has promoted love and concern for neighbour, and moral and spiritual progress) and 'Christendom' (the religious institutions and leadership which have had more than their share of responsibility for perpetuating injustices, starting holy wars, and sanctioning the laws of tyrants). Christians, in assessing the social-political relevance and viability of atheism, have to keep in mind the extreme relativity of the term 'atheism' – Christians themselves were officially designated as 'atheists' in the Roman Empire, whose official gods were impugned or ridiculed by Christians. And if we take into account such relativities, there is perhaps a point, as Teilhard de Chardin suggests,[15] at which the 'progressive' branch of Christianity will converge with the 'socially concerned' branch of atheism, so that the two will find themselves identical. The result would be no doubt at least democratic, perhaps something better.

The German philosopher Ernst Bloch tends towards even a stronger statement than Chardin: Not only can Christianity and atheism be compatible or 'converge', but they positively *need* each other. As Bloch puts it, 'only an atheist can be a good Christian; only a Christian can be a good atheist'.[16] Bloch speaks from the vantage point of a

Marxist who laments the loss in Marxism of the eschatological viewpoint and the commitment to a transcendent 'kingdom of God', a commitment which is found only in biblical Christianity and which paradoxically (if only Christians would realise it) might finally be implemented in the practical realm with the help of the technical and political–economic expertise of Marxist socialism. A proponent of 'Western' democracy might formulate a hypothesis similar to Bloch's with a different emphasis. He might ask: can the commitment to individualism which characterises so much of 'Western' democratic atheism flourish or even exist without that sense of the absolute uniqueness of the person which has been a heritage of Christianity? And is it not possible that a Christianity which has in the past concentrated overmuch on fulfilment in an 'afterlife' might paradoxically find the transcendent enrichment it was looking for by intensified concentration on maximum fulfillment of individual potential in *this life* (which, after all, was supposed to be, even for Christians, the germ or seed of any afterlife which might follow it)? Bloch's vision of a synthesis of 'Western' Christianity and Marxism, and the two sharply divergent versions of 'democracy' which have become associated with these two camps, is no doubt utopian – although eminent thinkers and activists in South American countries are currently involved in trying to forge just such a synthesis. But Christianity's main contribution to defusing hostilities between contemporary champions of 'democracy' may lie in implementing some of its more traditional goals: turning 'swords into ploughshares', promoting 'peace on earth', and relying more on the spiritual power generated by social justice than on military power for success and security.

NOTES

1. Arnold Brecht, *Political Theory*, pp. 456–76.
2. G. W. F. Hegel, *Philosophy of History*, Sibree tr. (NY: Dover, 1956), p. 51.
3. Ibid., pp. 50–1, pp. 444–5. The free state that Hegel envisages is Lutheran and proudly nationalistic. The limitations of Hegel's vision are perhaps adumbrated by the fact that in the 1930s in Germany it was the traditionally nationalistic Protestants who put Hitler into power. Catholics, from various motivations, were disinclined to support Hitler, as Richard Hamilton shows in *Who Voted for Hitler* (Princeton University Press, 1982).
4. See *The Protestant Ethic and the Spirit of Capitalism*, Parsons tr. (London, 1930) *passim*.

5. Sacvan Bercovitch, *The Puritan Origins of the American Self* (New Haven: Yale University Press, 1975).
6. See Carl J. Friedrich, *Man and His Government*, ch. VI; and *Transcendent Justice: The Religious Dimensions of Constitutionalism*, ch. I.
7. For a detailed study of these influences, see *Religion and the American Mind*, by Alan E. Heimert (Mass.: Harvard University Press, 1967).
8. Here it should be mentioned that – especially if we assume that religion and politics are two separate and independent spheres – the comparative maladaptability of Catholicism to democracy does not necessarily imply that Catholicism is in any way inferior to Protestantism (even if democracy were the best form of government, it is conceivable that a 'democratic' *religion* might not be the best form of religion).
9. See e.g. *Two Cheers for Capitalism* (NY: Basic Books, 1977) and 'The Death of the Socialist Idea', *Saturday Evening Post*, March 1979.
10. B. F. Skinner's *Beyond Freedom and Dignity* may be taken as an illustration of the way in which atheistic-materialist premises can lead logically to conclusions downgrading traditional democratic valuations of personal dignity as well as freedom.
11. See Sartre's 'La fantome de Staline' in *Situations VII* (Paris: Gallimard, 1965).
12. E.g. in his *Critique of Dialectical Reason* (1960), his Preface to Franz Fanon's *Wretched of the Earth* (1961); in 'Capitulation ou contre-escalede', in *Les Temps Modernes*, 242 (1966) pp. 193–6; and 'Conversation with Jean-Paul Sartre', in *Oui* 4 (1975) pp. 123f.
13. *Democracy in America*, p. 151.
14. Or at least superhuman. Some ideas of God do not seem to involve infinity in the strict sense. However, a basic epistemological question arises here as to whether anyone, theist or atheist, can excogitate the finite without having also some vague concept of an outlying infinite – either the infinity of God, or the infinite perfectibility of the human race, or the infinite importance of the self or ego.
15. Teilhard de Chardin's projection of such a merger in *The Future of Man* (New York: Harper & Row, 1964) ch. XVIII.
16. See the frontispiece of Bloch's *Atheism in Christianity*, Swann tr. (NY: Herder & Herder, 1972).

9 The Future of Democracy in the International Sphere

How then are we to have order in the international field? How can we secure the reign of one law over all the people of several nations? Only if they, the people, freely endow an agency of their own with the function of making the rules and the power to enforce the rules. These, as we have seen, are uses of the sovereignty that abides in men, not in the state.

Can the citizens of an autocracy and those of a democracy jointly create such an agency? No one has yet shown how they can. For an autocrat speaks and acts, not as agent for his people, but as their ruler. He is sovereign and independent. He can make a treaty, though his subjects do not want it. He can cancel or disregard that treaty, though his subjects wish to keep it. . . .

Contrast the case of a democracy. The people may irrevocably agree that they shall be bound by the rules made by their own agency – the government they erect.

National sovereignty is the enemy of international law. Its affirmation is the negation of law above the national level.

Publius II, *The New Federalist*, no. 3

The atomic warfare of the future puts a life-or-death premium on secrecy in preparation and surprise attack. In every war, the initial advantage is to dictatorships rather than democracies, because they can proceed without popular discussion or consent; but in the next war, the initial advantage will also be the final one.

Mortimer Adler, 'A Disputation on the Future of Democracy'

When those of us who live in what we call 'democratic' countries try to excogitate our future role in the international scene, it is impossible for us to do so without, at least implicitly, conceiving some specific model of world order as the backdrop or context of our thinking. But since 'Western' civilisation has not developed any positive, well-defined, and universally accepted ideology, but formulates what ideology it has in a vague and negativistic way (as the champions of the 'right of self-determination as opposed to communist collectivism'), it is not surprising that we find it hard to come up with a definite ideal, when we are pressed to do so. (Well-read Communists, on the other hand, can give decisive and fairly uniform 'scientific' answers when subjected to such challenges.) In general we seem to tend to project or extrapolate the systems that we already have and are familiar with into the international sphere (such that internationalism becomes our own society, 'writ large'). Thus Woodrow Wilson, in his architectonic for the makeup of the incipient League of Nations, envisaged only 'democratic' countries as full-fledged members. As the League developed, it gradually relaxed its restrictions on membership. The United Nations finally, as successor to the League, tried to define conditions for membership as broadly as possible, by developing a charter of basic rights to which many countries which were not specifically democratic (in our sense) could subscribe. Like the World Council of Churches, the end result of the United Nations has been an impressive external structural unity hiding apparently irreconcilable differences in policy and unbridgeable ideological rifts. For example, the United States seems to imagine the future of the world as a gigantic reproduction of its own federal union of diverse and independent states, while the USSR is working towards a completely different model, a new world empire with centralised authority administered under a new version of 'divine right'.[1] Outside the porticos of the UN, international relations and diplomatic negotiations are hampered by a similar lack of understanding and consensus concerning ideals. As Henry Kissinger once observed, the tendency of 'Western' oriented countries to try to manipulate world realities after the prototype of their own bureaucratic-pragmatic domestic structures, coupled with the countervailing tendencies (a) of bureaucratic ideological nations such as the USSR, and (b) of certain revolutionary–ideological nations in the 'third world' – present a continuing obstacle to the emergence of any stable international order.[2] Adam Ulam strikes a similar note in a recent article which describes the continuing impasse resulting from the attempts of a relatively decentralised government such as that of the US trying to negotiate with an autocratic country like the USSR whose motives are often intentionally inscrutable:

> Quite aside from the concrete issues separating them, it is the very nature of their general approach to foreign policy that makes it so hard for the United States and the Soviet Union to carry on a meaningful diplomatic dialogue, let alone solve some of their outstanding differences. On the Soviet side, the obsessive secrecy in which decision-making is veiled and the camouflage thrown over their real hopes and fears, and, on the US side, the excessive volatility of American foreign policy and the diffusion of responsibility for its conduct, combine to undermine that mutual credibility which is a basic condition of fruitful negotiations. It is as difficult for the Americans to believe Soviet promises as it is for the Kremlin to heed seriously the US government's warnings.[3]

In spite of the sharp East–West disparity of goals and the blatant lack of consensus about the *kind* of world order which should emerge, the difficulties of only several decades ago, concerning whether any world order is necessary *at all*, are beginning to dissolve. In a prenuclear age, it was easy for the US Senate to muster opposition against official US participation in the League of Nations, and to effectively block its membership; and it sounded reasonable for a respected thinker like John Dewey to conjecture that peace could be maintained without any world federation, if only the great powers would declare war illegal and agree to prosecute any offending (war-making) countries. Nuclear power, however, and the threat of nuclear extinction, even for countries using such power for 'just' causes, has not only introduced a qualitative change into war-making but, as Morganthau observes, has radically altered notions of foreign policy and international relations since the beginning of history.[4] In spite of centuries of explicit or implicit allegiance to 'anarchic' principles governing the relationship between nations, there seems to be a consensus emerging in only the last few decades on the necessity for some stable and dependable structure of world order – which at its maximum can mean a centralized world government, and at its minimum various conceptions of a quasi-institutionalised 'balance of power'.

The trend in theories of international relations at present is to focus on the functional interactions taking place worldwide in terms of clusters of processes rather than in terms of entitative national units and any structural organisation obtaining among them. But, although such attention to processes per se may be a useful instrument for overcoming attitudinal 'blocks' or presuppositions for the scientist who is trying to determine 'what is going on' in the world at large, it is not psychologically possible to consider such processes in *complete* abstraction from the context of entitative national structures from which the processes are emerging or towards which they are tending (a good analogue would be the relationship between function and structure in the human embryo). In our philosophical consideration of the future functions of democracy in the world order (a consideration which implies an 'ought') the best approach would seem to be an analysis and comparison of the main projections of the sort of world order towards which we are tending, with a view to coming to understand the hierarchy of options in terms of the requirements of democratic government. The main conceptions now seem to be three in number: (1) a world government; (2) minimal international organisation, a self-regulating 'balance of power' mechanism substituting for such organisation; and (3) an international federation of nations.

A HIGHLY CENTRALISED WORLD GOVERNMENT

Arnold Toynbee in his *Study of History* points out frequently that 'universal states' *de facto* have served the purpose of enforcing worldwide peace. Many Western political theorists from the fourteenth-century monarchist Dante Alighieri to the twentieth-century left-wing radical philosopher Bertrand Russell have theorised that the final attainment of peace among sovereign nations would require some kind of central authority imposing peace by force. The nature of this envisaged authority seems to vary largely in correspondence with the opinions of individuals concerning the best *domestic* type of government – in Dante's case, the preference was for a monarchy, in Russell's for a non-communist but sufficiently socialist and labour-oriented leader-nation or -nations. The main proponents in our day of a strong and (if necessary) violent imposition of a central authority on the rest of the world are Marxist Leninists, according to whose worldview the present oppression of the 'proletarian' nations of the world (including the Soviet Union!) by the capitalist countries must be reversed through at least a temporary dictatorship under the direction of the proletariat (proletarian nations) until a worldwide classless society makes oppression a thing of the past. If, however, the Soviets, or any central authority were to try to subject a *nuclear* power to their rule by force, the results would probably be unimaginably catastrophic. Thus the suggestion of the British socialist politician John Strachey, in *On the Prevention of War* (1962), that the US and the Soviet Union should form a joint hegemony over the rest of the world, may not be as far-fetched as it sounds at first blush. The major apparent obstacle to such a hegemony would be the natural reluctance of a country like the US, which prides itself on being democratic, establishing anything like an old-fashioned empire by force. This reasoning and the feelings of reluctance, however, are not completely cogent, since as a matter of historical fact, many states, including many 'democratic' states, have been originally established by force. No doubt the objections of Soviet ideologists, in the minds of whom any such overt alliance with a major capitalist power would be treason to Marxist principles, would be stronger obstacles to such a hegemony. However, the US and the USSR have joined forces in the past to take *antidisruptive* action, e.g. in the 1956 Suez crisis; thus a future antidisruptive hegemony would have some precedent.

The only thing that could be stated with some degree of certainty about any possible future centralised world government including nuclear powers is that it could not be autocratic. It would be most probably administered by at least two leaders whose chief occupation, it seems, would be dividing power and jurisdictions between themselves on a day-to-day basis, as Roosevelt, Stalin and Churchill once did in an *ad hoc* fashion at Yalta. It also seems fairly certain that the only condition under which America's European allies would conceivably consent to such a hegemony would be a situation of an imminent worldwide nuclear holocaust – and even then European consent would not be guaranteed, even on a temporary basis.

On the purely theoretical level, Errol Harris conjectures that such a world government might be, ironically enough, the only way orthodox Marxism could ever surface. For, according to Marxist doctrine, the main conflict is an international struggle between classes. But the failure of workers throughout the world to unite has been explained away by the Marxists as a result of their 'seduction by the bourgeoisie'. As a result, we now hear about a war of 'socialist nations' against 'capitalist nations', instead of an authentic international class struggle: but a world government which de-emphasised present interpretations of national sovereignty, would indirectly *link* the workers of the various national units and make a bona fide international class struggle possible and even probable, thus vindicating Marx.[5]

A 'BALANCE OF POWER' STANDOFF

Many prefer to see the future world order in terms of a 'balance of power', which would amount to 'world *order*' only in the wide sense, i.e. insofar as it functions to prevent absolute disintegration or chaos on a worldwide scale. Alexis de Tocqueville seemed to have a prophetic inkling of what we now call the 'balance of power' when he observed (in the 1830s) that 'each of them [the United States and Russia] seems marked out by the will of Heaven to sway the destinies of half the globe'.[6] His powers of prophecy prove to be only incompletely accurate, however, when he indicates that this future division of power will be one in which 'the Anglo-American relies upon personal interest to accomplish his ends, and gives free scope to the unguided strength and common sense of the people; the Russian [in contrast] centres all the authority of society in a single arm. The principle instrument of the former is freedom; of the latter, servitude'. This is the way in which Americans would like to *see* their contribution to the 'balance of power' schema; and in the eyes of some Americans, who concentrate only selectively on items such as America's assistance to Europeans in fighting Nazism in World War II, or the highly successful Marshall Plan or 'lend lease' or the 'point four' programme after the war, Tocqueville's statement is an amazingly accurate prediction. But a more balanced view would have to consider US support of dictatorships in South Vietnam, South Korea, Greece, Iran, El Salvador and elsewhere, CIA activities in overthrowing democratically elected governments such as Allende's Chilean administration, and US assistance (through NATO) to France in preventing colonial independence in Vietnam and Algeria, to Portugal in keeping its colonies in Angola and Mozambique, to Belgium in the Congo, and to Britain for maintaining its power in Malaya, Kenya, and the Persian Gulf – leading to the conclusion that a major portion of US foreign policy is concerned with other objectives than 'supporting the cause of freedom and self-determination everywhere'. Excursions of both the US and the USSR into the realm of force, together with the incessant stockpiling of nuclear weapons, have transformed the 'balance of power' into what is called in more contemporary jargon the 'balance of terror', the ambivalent objective of which is to both prevent and guarantee MAD (Mutually Assured Destruction). It is not at all clear that this transformation is avoidable. As M. ten Hoor observes, the citizens of a democracy, adhering to *strict* democratic principles, preferring to 'live and let live' in the world as a whole, may not be able to survive in a world programmed for wars of aggression.[7] If Americans were so idealistic, for example, as only to accept aid from, and give military aid to, anticommunist nations which were democratic rather than dictatorial and which eschewed colonial imperialism, they might have found themselves with the 'wolf at the door' already. Whether or not democracy is the best form of government, it is not necessarily the most efficient government for waging war, even 'cold' wars or wars of self-defence. Thus there was a certain wisdom in President Ford's defence in 1975 of CIA activities – 'if other governments are resorting to these things, we have to follow suit'.

Some theorists see continuance of the present 'balance of terror' as a realistic and even *feasible* means of maintaining world order and peace in the future, through fear. Thus R. Aron in a kind of contemporary *Realpolitik* hypothesises that there is at present a dialectic of weaponry which is helping to maintain the world in a stable equilibrium and may continue to do so – nuclear weapons preventing world wars, conventional weapons (tanks, etc.) preventing local wars, and guerrilla weapons (e.g. the machine gun) preventing colonial domination of small and poor nations by outsiders.[8] Aron considers this 'anarchical order' of world power a possibly reasonable compromise between subjugation of individual nations to a world-state on the one hand, and annihilation in a nuclear war on the other.

Others consider such peace through terror and through war-making powers hardly any peace in the strict sense: two military forces continually massing against one another and adding weaponry to their already abundant supplies, for years and years, are certainly not at peace even if neither of them actually makes an attempt to fight and defeat the other. Earl Ravenal proposes that we renounce 'balance of power' objectives, which are now concerned mostly with 'overkill', and are totally maladapted to a nuclear age. We should concentrate instead, he says, on the preservation of domestic security and judicious adaptation to changes taking place in the world:

> The United States and the Soviet Union are . . . like two gigantesque sumo wrestlers, engaged only ostensibly in a wrestling contest but actually in an eating contest – and perhaps in a grunting contest. Does each competitor grow healthier as it grows fatter? Are their spectators, the rest of the world, supposed to be impressed and deferential?
>
> We have to challenge the very idea of military balance – not whether it happens to be in our favour, but whether we need a

> military balance at all, as opposed to the more limited notion of stability, which is quite essential.[9]

Nigel Calder in a recent book goes even further, suggesting that further continuance of MAD strategy is not only unwise, but meaningless, since MAD is only a viable strategy when countries must *choose* between hitting cities and hitting the enemy's weapons.[10] Now when both superpowers have an abundance of weapons, a victim whose land weapons had been destroyed, may *not* want to retaliate with air or submarine defences against the enemy's cities (a move which would instigate obliteration of his own cities).

Even if the MAD strategy has some validity, it seems that the 'race' with the USSR which it involves is to a great extent artificially stimulated by the American Arms Coalition's systematic misrepresentations of unbalance (e.g. calculating Soviet disbursements for soldiers' wages on the basis of wages paid to US soldiers), as Daniel Yergin has pointed out.[11]

If a group of inveterate enemies found themselves together in a situation of danger, and it became clear that none of them would come out alive unless all of them found a means to communicate and cooperate (at least temporarily), it is probable they would find such means after some preliminary hedging to 'save face'. If and when the danger of a nuclear catastrophe becomes *clear* and absolutely *concrete* (hopefully not by a repetition of Hiroshima and Nagasaki), it seems probable that the major powers will take steps to defuse the danger, at least by deescalation of armaments or control of nuclear testing. If the hostile nations prefer to maintain equilibrium through mutual fear and the 'balance of power', this negative and anarchistic sort of peacekeeping might, as Carl Friedrich points out, have even a greater chance of being successful if the balance of power is multipolar rather than bipolar.[12] Since it is not a question in a 'balance of power' model of choosing or voting for one of the contenders over the other, a relatively strong 'third party' (China?) would be performing a useful service if it might prohibit either of the other two parties *in perpetuum* from gaining the ascendancy.

AN INTERNATIONAL FEDERATION

In a 'liberal democracy' like the US, the extreme libertarian and also the dedicated anarchist – for both of whom the motto is 'the less government, the better' – since they cannot tolerate much government in the domestic sphere, will *a fortiori* be opposed to creating new governmental structures (and possibly bureaucracies) on a global basis. Even if one accepts their premises, however, one need not come to the same conclusions they come to. If one has a feeling for paradox, it is entirely conceivable that the net effect of world government would be to *loosen* the hold of each of the individual member governments over their respective citizens, as Publius II suggests in *The New Federalist.*[13] We might expect that liberals and moderates, unlike libertarians and anarchists, would, once they had come to the conviction that something had to take the place of worldwide fear, favour an international organization of nations which would itself be democratic in structure.[14] A citizen of the United States, which is a union or federation of 50 states, would no doubt conceive of a 'democratic' world government in terms of a parallel federation of the world's sovereign nations. Arnold Toynbee in *Experiences*[15] argues that such a federation could be a veritable key to peace in the contemporary world, since it would abolish that one-sided emphasis on local sovereignty that has been the traditional historical source of conflict among nation-states.

The United Nations at present is a miniscule approximation to such a federation. It has been an extraordinary political experiment insofar as it has involved bringing together within a Western *democratic* structure a group of nations, some of which do not believe in Western democracy and in fact would like to do away with it and substitute political structures that they find more comfortable. Because of such basic ideological disparity, the United Nations' General Assembly and Security Council are rather a quasi-confederation analogous to the US under the Articles of Confederation (1781–89), than an efficient organisation achieving much in the way of concerted action. To this day there has still been no magic metamorphosis from discussion to bona fide federal power. The closest the Security Council ever got to taking decisive 'governmental' action was in June 1950, when the Soviet Representative happened to be absent in protest against the inclusion of Nationalist China on the Security Council, and the Security Council for the first and only time was able to take prompt and decisive military action on a threat to world peace (the invasion of South Korea by North Korean forces) without a Soviet veto. However, the Soviet delegate returned shortly afterwards and prevented any substantial follow-up action in that particular emergency, and the Soviet delegates have maintained excellent attendance records since then. Shortly afterward, the General Assembly tried to devise ways of bypassing or counterbalancing such a future impasse in the Security Council, but has been able to attain only intermittent unanimity in defusing conflicts (when the principal powers have to tolerate UN intervention), hardly any dependable effectiveness.

Such wholly predictable and expectable inability of the UN to attain anything like a government-with-sanctions should incite us to seriously re-examine the wisdom of trying to establish a quasi-democratic international body without having as a prerequisite some sort of homogeneity in attitudes and a basic sympathy to liberal democratic structures among the constituent nations. Would it not have been better for the world, in the aftermath of World War II, to set up a more limited United Nations (after the original Wilsonian pattern) consisting only of the US and its allies and any nation, large or small, which satisfied certain conditions as to democratic structures? It is conceivable that, with such a consensus, more decisive action might have been taken in the various crises which have arisen in Southeast Asia, the Middle East, Africa, the Baltic countries and elsewhere, and that even now something like a governmental federation of friendly Western nations and their allies might be functioning effectively, might have swung the balance of power strongly in the direction of Western democracy, and might be evolving with some celerity in the direction of a world federation 'with teeth'.

If the better part of realism leads us to accept the UN 'as is', and capitalise on whatever virtues it has, we must be honest enough to recognise the sharp limitations of the UN in providing a base for any future democratically oriented federation of governments. As long as there exist major powers within the UN with ideologies officially inimical to the existence and progress of Western democracy, there can only be a pseudo-federation, at most an international confederation enormously sophisticated in diplomacy and protocol. *If* the communist powers now on the Security Council were to retract their dogmas concerning the inevitability of worldwide communist domination, and to proffer a more moderate ideology which envisioned communism as just one among several viable political systems in the world, *then* the United States and other similarly inclined nations might begin to function as a gigantic 'political party' in the world as a whole, fostering the cause of the rights of the individual and the individual nation (just as certain political parties now consider themselves champions of the individual) in constructive opposition to the communist 'party' which, presumably, would defend the rights of the community or collectivity and the international community of workers with equal ardour.

Actually such a partisan attempt at establishing political territoriality is taking place at present in the UN, but not exactly in accord with the 'script' just suggested, and not exactly with the 'sporting' attitude often characterising rivalries between established political parties. The countries of the 'third world' (sometimes the undeveloped countries are distinguished into a 'third' and '*fourth*' world on the basis of the presence or absence of national resources), growing more and more numerous in the UN, have in the name of Third World opposition learned how to outvote and supervene the US and its allies in important strategic matters. Daniel Moynihan, the US Ambassador to the UN during 1975–76, writes, 'If the debates of the League of Nations in Geneva of the late 1930's had a certain irrelevance about them, they were nonetheless led by democratic statesmen. But by the early 1970's the scene at the United Nations was very different. The world organisation was growing in membership and in a certain kind of ideological authority, and this new strength was increasingly deployed on behalf of totalitarian principles and practiced wholly at variance with its original purpose.'[16] In view of the impasse which has been reached, Moynihan has suggested that the time has come for the liberal democratic constituency to realise it is now becoming a 'minority' force, and, in accord with that realisation, to take on a kind of parliamentary role as the 'loyal opposition'.[17]

This is certainly not the sort of development that Franklin D. Roosevelt or Winston Churchill had in mind when they participated in the Yalta Conference in 1945 and concluded the final agreements establishing the UN as a permanent organisation. No doubt Stalin himself was also contemplating quite a different scenario from the one that has occurred. It is possible, however, that in view of the weakening of the position of the US, the Soviets and their allies may pragmatically but drastically change their attitude towards 'democracy', and begin in earnest to make new efforts to overthrow the power of 'imperialism' or capitalism by 'democratic' means – lobbying, voting, caucusing, securing representation, asking for referenda and recall or their equivalents, etc. (now that such methods are apt to achieve better results than brute force and dialectical materialism). If this takes place, will not the United States and its allies begin to have significant misgivings about the efficacy and progressiveness of 'democratic' processes?

The *de facto* 'model' realistic Westerners and pragmatic communists are working with now seems to be the 'balance of power' model. A tripartite balance of power, with mainland China as the leader of the Third World, may be an effective model for defusing aspirations for world domination, provided that we are willing to live indefinitely with the fear of the 'outside possibility' of a surprise nuclear attack from another major power or from some guerrilla organisation which manages to acquire and put together the ingredients for a plutonium bomb. If this is not satisfactory, if our objective is to get out from under the constant threat of destruction or annihilation (and here there is a *striking* analogue to the Hobbesian theory about the fear of death leading to the formation of political entities in the first place), some sort of stable international political structure will have to be formed. The democratic, federative model that the US proponents of the United Nations had in mind seems ironically (if the UN may be taken as a possible seminal beginning of some future full-fledged federation) to be working *counter* to the interests of what we call democracy. The more autocratic highly centralised model, ruling by force by a single nation, is at present unacceptable to the United States (because of moral qualms), as well as impossible to achieve because of shifts in the balance of power during the 1960s and 1970s; it is also impossible for the Soviet Union to achieve, because of similar limitations in power. It is conceivable that, with the emergence of 'third world' politics, the US and the USSR may overcome some of the ideological differences or moral qualms they may have, to establish a hegemony over the rest of the world before any other nations become major nuclear powers. At the present time it would seem that either this latter model or the 'balance of terror' model would offer the only realistic context for our thinking about the role of a democracy like the US in the world of the future. Both models, however, would seem to compromise democracy: hegemony, because world-rule by a democracy would create a schizophrenia between domestic democracy and international despotism; the 'balance of terror', because the complexities of nuclear defence or retaliation by a democratic power have already become so formidable that they have been taken out of human hands (both military and civilian) and relegated to computers – e.g., the Single Integrated Operating Plan (SIOP) computer (programmed with secret options, none of which involve surrender) at the US Strategic Air Command headquarters in Omaha, Nebraska.

With an accent on optimism, however, there are three possible 'scenarios' conceivable in view of the three models we have been discussing:

FIRST SCENARIO

The US and Russia, reacting to the building up of nuclear power in China, Israel, the Arab bloc, or guerrilla groups, and possibly also to threats of territorial infringements with more conventional weapons and terrorist attacks, decide for 'the good of the world' (and perhaps with the consent of smaller nations which have suffered nuclear disasters or have been exposed to nuclear threats) to form a hegemony over the rest of the world, involving stringent inspection and control of subordinate societies. If guerrilla warfare became rampant, a universal imperialistic 'police state' would be required to combat it. Cooperation between the two great powers would doubtlessly be facilitated not only by increased economic and cultural exchange, but also by the fact that 'the real enemy' had proven to be some third party outside the orbit of either political system. The unity of the two countries in this scenario is conceivable not in terms of submission of both to some single political executive, or even to a joint executive power, but mainly in terms of union for specific military and policing functions, perhaps under a single commander (although the difficult and uneasy alliance of American, British and Soviet forces under Eisenhower in the final stages of World War II offers only a weak precedent for such an eventuality).

SECOND SCENARIO

A continuation of the 'balance of power' syndrome is also conceivable, complete with regular and ritualised negotiations about armament (never complete disarmament) to keep mutual fear down to an acceptable minimum. This solution would be severely challenged, however, by the acquisition of plutonium bombs by guerrilla groups, and/or by internal economic problems making defence spending more and more of a burden in the major nuclear nations. From the point of view of *US* security, this scenario might be the most feasible one, provided that (1) the current trend to increase the accuracy of US missiles continues, involving e.g. American ability to hit Soviet missile silos; (2) Americans surrounded themselves either with a high technology 'great wall' consisting of an antiballistic system manned with laser beams, gamma rays and X-rays, and/or with a multilayer 'High Frontier' satellite missile defence (as recently proposed by the Heritage Foundation), in order to defend themselves against Soviet missiles headed for American cities; (3) European allies continued to support NATO missile installations at a sufficient level; and (4) Americans refused to supply the Soviets with the additional computers, sensors, and communications systems they need to overcome their own lag in information technology and to make contemplated advances in nuclear armaments. If Americans reached this stage in armament, it would seem useless and possibly economically suicidal to continue developments of nuclear firepower for destroying Soviet *cities*. The chief weakness of this scenario so far is that, in the absence of any sacrosanct defence alliance or federation, it would presumably leave many Western allies just as vulnerable to obliteration as they now are. The 'happy ending' in this scenario comes when and if, impelled by fear and futility, the superpowers finally enter into serious agreements to halt nuclear *testing* (which, if verification is adequate, could bring a terminus to the arms race, since deployment of new weaponry without testing would eventually prove precarious).

THIRD SCENARIO

The Communist bloc and the Third World, just beginning to understand what they can accomplish by 'democracy' in the UN, and perhaps also discovering in their own domestic economics and politics that a certain modicum of 'liberal democracy' is required to pursue their socialist objectives efficiently, may begin to pursue their national and international objectives in more 'democratic' ways, through compromise, negotiations, alliances, friendly but well-organised competition with 'opposition parties', etc., and thus eventually find themselves, through a kind of political 'osmosis', operating with basically democratic tactics. The US and some Western democracies, at the same time, may find themselves in such severe economic straits, with scarcities, inflation, deficits and recession or depression, that they have to begin to ape the 'planned economies' of their communist competitors and sharply curtail political freedom as we know it now. Simultaneously the Western democracies may begin to 'caucus' more regularly among themselves – for example, in economic summits – thus developing a 'united front' against the 'Eastern Bloc'.[18] Parallel to the dynamics found in many domestic two-party systems competing for votes from their electorate, the two contending alliances competing for the allegiance of neutral or marginal or Third World nations may begin to avoid ideological extremes and edge towards middle-of-the-road positions. This third scenario envisions a gradual simplification of the world hostilities into two opposite camps which evolve from hostility to 'loyal opposition', and which may be able to establish a limited world federation, to which qualified outlying nations could apply for membership at any time. This scenario implies that it may be naive to work simply for 'world unity'. The necessary and sufficient basis for the attainment of world unity may be the clarification and perpetuation of some natural and ineluctable divisions in the world system, which are beginning to make themselves manifest.

* * *

On the basis of purely political prognostication, the future of democratic foreign policy and international relations does not look too bright. But in thinking about political possibilities, we tend to abstract from social, economic, and cultural concomitants; and this may be a mistake. These other factors may, indeed, be theoretically separable from political considerations, but *in concreto* have all the relevance in the world to political formations. If, perhaps, in a kind of despair at ever attaining a world government, the advocates of world government were to resolve to concentrate their energies on various aspects of 'apolitical' international unification – e.g. the overcoming of language barriers, the attainment of universal literacy and basic worldwide standards of living (the UN already has committees 'breaking ground' in these areas), the institutionalisation of regular athletic competition in a wide variety of popular sports, and/or the transcendence of religious differences – the result might be the paradoxical attainment, by gradual evolutionary processes, of the goal which they had previously despaired of attaining. Thus, to take just one example, it is obvious that the present-day multiplicity of religions in both the Western and the Eastern worlds would be a divisive factor and an obstacle to any group or agency trying to establish either a highly centralised government or a governmental federation of nations. In view of this, there is a certain logic in Karl Marx's insistence on the necessity of doing away with religion as a preamble to establishing a universal communist social order; and, on the other side, it is understandable why the renowned historian Arnold Toynbee attaches particular importance in the post-World War II world to the possible unifying function of a single world religion (he has in mind the Christian religion) for supplying the impetus to the formation of a new 'civilisation'.[19] It is hard to conceive, however, how changes in the Christian religion or any other religion might have any effect, one way or the other, on the Soviet Union or Communist China. It is more probable that some very 'secular' syntheses in *philosophy* or ideology may be more important – e.g. the principle that individual freedom and the socialisation of man are *equally* important values, and thus must *both* be preserved in any socio-political schema (a simple intuition that would seem to have a chance of 'carrying both houses', except that 'floor fights' would inevitably break out when it came to defining 'freedom' and 'socialisation'.) Debates on a strictly philosophical level about controversial matters can indeed be unsettling and even destabilising, but they are usually bloodless; and when they are accompanied by a belief in, and the pursuit of, truth, they often help clear the air and sometimes pave the way for solutions. In particular, in a busy world in which philosophical questions about democracy have taken a backseat to practical disputes and open hostilities among various contenders for 'democracy', the temporary retirement from the hustle and bustle of cold and hot warfare to consider pivotal philosophical issues may be necessary for achieving a tolerable unanimity. We tend to think, 'let's get together in praxis, and then we can discuss the philosophical issues'; but, on both the individual and the collective level, things often proceed the other way around.

NOTES

1. Carl Friedrich, *Man and His Government*, p. 577.
2. 'Domestic Structure and Foreign Policy', *Daedalus* (Journal of the American Academy of Arts and Sciences), xcv, 2, Spring 1966, pp. 503–24.
3. Adam Ulam, 'U.S.–Soviet Relations: Unhappy Coexistence', in *Foreign Affairs*, vol. 57, no. 3, 1979.
4. *The Decline of Democratic Politics* (University of Chicago Press, 1962) p. 11.
5. See *Annihilati n and Utopia* (London: Allen & Unwin, 1966) p. 285.
6. *Democracy in America*, p. 142
7. *Freedom Limited*, p. 183.
8. 'The Anarchical Order of Power', *Daedalus*, xcv, 2, Spring 1966, pp. 479–501.
9. See 'How to Cut the Defense Budget', *Inquiry*, 1 May 1978, p. 20.
10. *Nuclear Nightmares: an Investigation into Possible Wars* (NY: Viking, 1980). President Carter's 1980 presidential directive (P.D. 59) allows theoretically for a move away from civilian to military and political targets; but strategists seem wary of sacrificing the immense *psychologica* deterrent-possibilities of MAD by proclaiming a more selective 'sane' nuclear strategy.

11. See Daniel Yergin, 'The Arms Zealots', *Harpers*, June 1977.
12. *Man and His Government*, p. 673.
13. See *The New Federalist* (NY: Harper, 1950) pp. 17–18. In arguing that federal union would help decentralise the governments of component nation-states, Publius II is here following the lead of Publius I (Hamilton & Madison). See *The Federalist*, papers No. 10 and No. 16.
14. See ten Hoor, *Freedom Limited*, p. 214.
15. Arnold Toynbee, *Experiences* (Oxford University Press, 1969).
16. Quoted by Tom Bethell in 'The Diplomat's Disease', *Washington Monthly*, March 1979.
17. 'The U.S. in Opposition', in *Commentary*, March 1975, LX, 1.
18. The final recommendations offered by Stanley Hoffmann in *Primacy of World Order: American Foreign Policy Since the Cold War* (NY: McGraw Hill, 1978) tend in this direction. Hoffmann suggests that the US work primarily towards forming 'coalitions' of friendly and neutral nations pursuing matters of mutual self-interest whether within the UN or outside of that body. Ray S. Cline, in 'A New Grand Strategy for the United States: an Essay', in *Comparative Strategy*, I, 1 and 2, 1978, is even more specific. He suggests a ten-nation 'Oceans Alliance' of the US, Canada, West Germany, France, Britain, Israel, Japan, the Republic of China/Taiwan, and Australia – perhaps augmented with a secondary thirteen-nation alliance of Mexico, Spain, etc. The Trilateral plan proposed by Jimmy Carter, Zbigniew Brzezinski, et al. proposes a multi-phase approximation to world-community, beginning with (1) the US, Western Europe and Japan, then incorporating (2) Australia, Israel, Mexico and other developed countries, then (3) Yugoslavia, Romania, and other progressive communist countries, and then finally (4) all the nations of Latin America, Africa and Asia. The catalyst for stability under the Trilateral plan would not be 'balance of power' but new applications of political economics to world problems. (In view of the ongoing Marxist incursions in Africa and Latin America, it is becoming doubtful that phase # 4 of the Trilateral plan could ever be implemented.)
19. See *A Study of History* (London: Oxford University Press, 1972) vol. VII, p. 555.

10 Is Democracy the Best Form of Government?

Do democracies make more and greater mistakes than other forms of government? . . . Is not illegal lynching a lesser evil than legal liquidation? What is the difference between slavery, which the democracies abolished, and the labor camps which Soviet Russia has instituted? If we compare the (alleged) low level of universal education in American democracy with the high level of the selective aristocratic system in some European democracies, which is to be preferred? This being settled, how does the favored system compare in promise for humanity with the controlled system of education in Communist Russia?

M. ten Hoor, *Freedom Limited*

[The 'old' liberals, who were suspicious of interference from government in the affairs of the citizenry] had no glimpse of the fact that private control of the new forces of production, forces which affect the life of everyone, would operate in the same way as private unchecked control of political power. They saw the need for new legal institutions, and of different political conditions as a means to political liberty. But they failed to perceive that social control of economic forces is equally necessary if anything approaching economic equality and liberty is to be realised.

John Dewey, *Liberalism and Social Action* (1935)

The terrifying phenomenon of totalitarianism, which has been born into our world perhaps four times, did not issue from authoritarian systems, but in each case from a weak democracy: the one created by the February Revolution in Russia, the Weimar and the Italian Republics, and Chiang Kai-shek's China.

Aleksandr Solzhenitsyn, 'Misconceptions about Russia'

In posing again the traditional question about the 'best form of government', we might take a lead (this time around) from an idea prevalent in a philosophical movement which is not expressly political – the phenomenological movement. Husserl, Heidegger, Sartre and other exponents of 'phenomenology' (or 'existential phenomenology'), although they disagree about many things, seem to concur in at least one important insight: there is no possibility of studying consciousness in and for itself; consciousness is always consciousness-*of* something. In a somewhat parallel fashion, most people in our relativistic social milieu would be inclined to assent to the proposition that there is no validity to the pursuit of an 'absolutely best' form of government; in other words, a government can be adjudged 'best' only insofar as it is best-*for* the people who are governed.

But when it comes to deciding what *is* best-for the people, it is hard to maintain a pure 'relativist' position,[1] and the old absolute/relative dichotomy emerges again, since there is still the unresolved question concerning who will decide what is best-for the people – the experts and leaders, or the people themselves. The best government for the people might, on the one hand, be conceived as an updated version of the Platonic meritocracy, with governing officials chosen on the basis of tests for IQ, aptitude, values, and proven achievement and efficiency, and the proponent of such a government would rest secure in the conviction that, with such an aristocracy of talent and expertise, the governors in question will surely know what is best for the government in question, even if by some chance the majority of their citizens should be radically opposed to the type of government they are subjected to. On the other hand, the best government for the people might also be conceived as government *by* the people in the strict sense, i.e. a relatively best working organisation which will enable less-than-ideal, ordinary people to obtain to a great extent what they actually want, whether or not this happens to be best for them.[2]

Thus even among those committed to supporting the best government *for* the people, it is sometimes hard to maintain a pure and healthy relativism. For example, a theorist with internationalist leanings might prefer to define the best form of government in terms of the requirements for homeostasis in the 'world as a whole'. This sounds relativistic; but since the theory implies that a national leader would be making internationalist-oriented decisions not necessarily in line with the actual wishes of the people of his nation, this is simply a covert variation in the attempt to determine the absolute best for the people concerned. Or again, when ethicist John Rawls in his *Theory of Justice* (1971) theorises that an 'equilibrium state' should be built up around the concept of equilibrium between present generations and future generations, this sounds like a relativistic approach (devising a state which is best for people of all generations), but since we have no precise knowledge of what will be necessities and luxuries in future generations, such a theory has an absolutistic element about it, as Hubbard has argued.[3]

The idealistic–élitist notion that some talented men may know what constitutes the public welfare better than the public knows this itself may well have some truth to it. But, as Carl Cohen points out,[4] it also has a basic defect insofar as it presumes there is some 'independent welfare separable from the reality and purposes of its human citizens', i.e. *all* the subjects of a government. Those who consider this position untenable, or even repugnant, will tend, in spite of the difficulties and ambiguities mentioned above, towards the more 'relative' view that governments should be tailored to 'the people', whatever may be their foibles or defects.

But, going beyond mere foibles and defects – what if the 'people' are positively perverse or hopelessly ignorant or uneducated, or notoriously incompetent? Would it not be better for *such* people to have a less 'democratic', more authoritarian or paternalistic type of government? In a question like this lies a challenge to our faith (if we have it) in the 'average person'. Those who, upon introspection, discover that they really do not have much faith in the average person in a particular polity, will logically come to the conclusion that it would be better, at least in that particular case, if the control of the government were taken out of the hands of the average person. On the other hand, those who have a great confidence in the basic goodness and competence of the so-called 'average' person will gravitate towards a government which places maximum control in the hands of the general populace.

Aware of the importance of such subjective elements, some political philosophers – in an interesting reversal of the approach of Plato in the *Republic*, who tried to throw light on the notion of justice in the individual soul by concentrating on justice 'writ large' in the state – have tried to throw light on the ambivalences prevalent in democracy by using a psychological model emphasising common attitudes towards a distinction between a stronger and weaker, or better and worse, 'self' in the individual. Thus Carl Cohen[5] suggests that our conception of democracy runs parallel to our conception of the strength or weakness of the 'self': those who conceive the individual 'governing self' as lording it over itself (self-*determination* in the strict sense) are apt to emphasise centralisation and bureaucracy in a democracy; while those who conceive the 'governing self' as merely directing or 'steering' itself will emphasise grass-roots, participatory democracy receiving a minimum of administrative coordination from above. In a similar way Roberto Ungar[6] suggests that the common conception of the psyche as dichotomised into reason vs. desire and universal vs. particular is reflected in the common philosophical view of our democratic system as one which is plagued by 'inevitable' conflicts between 'ought' and 'is', between universal rules and individual evaluations. Jean Jacques Rousseau long ago drew a similar parallel between individual psyche and body politic, with a view to determining the proper direction of democratic government. According to Rousseau, there is in each man a division between the true self and the 'fitful' self, and any thinking person (reasons Rousseau) will allow that 'self-rule' in a democratic government should mean that the true (or better) self prevails over the fitful self. Rousseau was optimistic enough about the possibility of reconciling or coordinating these two 'selves' in a democracy as long as the democratic state was on a relatively small scale, e.g. ancient Athens or eighteenth-century Geneva. But he despaired of the possibility of such a synthesis being achieved in very large governments. In large 'democracies', social unity (the *res republica*) becomes a problem and can be maintained only by means of a dictatorship (such that 'natural liberty' becomes sacrificed for moral liberty-under-law and for the equality that results when the *res publica* is affirmed over each and every citizen). From this Rousseauan example it is easy to see why anyone who (consciously or unconsciously) thinks of both psyche and polity as involved in a 'better–worse' dichotomy, and also perceives the immense difficulty of subordinating worse to better on a very large scale, might lean towards an authoritarian government as the government that is best for the 'better man' within us all, as a government that requires 'the people' to rise up to its standards rather than stooping to some common denominator of popular standards, desires, and demands.

It is conceivable and even likely that most of the contemporary totalitarian 'democracies' were following some such logic in doing away with what Rousseau would call 'natural liberties': if every man were to buy and trade and speak and associate as he wills, it would be impossible to maintain cohesiveness and strict democratic equality among millions of citizens; let us, therefore (they conclude), establish a dictatorship to assure that reason and virtue will reign supreme and that the chaos and capriciousness of individual desires will never get out of hand. But as Yves Simon very acutely observed,[7] those who try in the name of 'true scientific socialism' or any other 'ism' to do away with the vagaries of fortune and the unpredictability of individual citizens by inaugurating a dictatorship, are in reality just establishing in place of the old species of chance another and possibly more menacing type – the possible and probable capriciousness of any individual who is given a *carte blanche* of control over the lives and fortunes of others. If we seriously consider this latter possibility, we will perhaps be the more amenable to accepting a good deal of individualistic or capitalistic capriciousness as a trade-off for the great and indubitable advantage of preventing (by means of regular elections and other democratic apparatus) the possibility of our becoming subject to the capriciousness or even charisma of some entrenched totalitarian leader.

It is certainly possible that in a situation where there are manageable numbers and an extraordinary sense of unity or camaraderie, a people may function quite well and even thrive without any strong centralised authority (Thomas Jefferson thought this was the case with many American Indian tribes in his time). It is also quite possible that a given people may be so rude, uncivilised, and untrustworthy that an autocratic or even despotic system might be best for them (Montesquieu and J. S. Mill, who preferred democratic or constitutional government, nevertheless favoured such autocratic systems in such limited cases). But as we have seen, the situation of most people, and our experiential observation of their situation, seems to be of the 'mixed variety – with the consequence that one seeking a political solution would tend neither towards pure decentralised capitalistic chaos nor a more covert arbitrariness in the guise of dictatorial control. It is perhaps because of a realistic assessment of this common experience that some political philosophers have vacillated with regard to their recommendations regarding 'the best possible government'. Thus, for example, Plato in the *Republic* opted for a communistic meritocracy, but later in the *Laws* tends towards the opinion that the best form of government would be an admixture of what is best in monarchy, aristocracy *and* democracy; Aristotle thought monarchy was the ideal, but ended up in his *Politics* recommending a mixture of democracy and oligarchy ('oligarchy', as Aristotle understood it, signified the political power of the propertied élite). Many contemporary thinkers seem to tend towards a similar 'mixed government' model when they approve a Madisonian style compromise between élitism and popular control of the state,[8] or a compromise between order and rationality on the one hand, and on the other, the capriciousness and disorder that one must make allowance for in dealing with ordinary human beings.[9]

American democracy, like many European democracies, is already such a compromise between the two complementary polar tendencies, the 'pure democratic' egalitarian trend and the quasi-aristocratic 'republican'[10] trend. These trends do not run strictly along party lines. A New Deal 'liberal' in the Democratic Party who wants to achieve equality by strong centralised bureaucratic administration rather than 'grass-roots' participation is speaking the language of the élitist who is basically distrustful of the ability of people to do things for themselves; and the grass-roots 'libertarian'[11] in the Republican Party who is distrustful of excessive corporate profits and 'welfare' for the rich, and wants to further the cause of the private citizen and the small businessman, is a liberal in libertarian clothing. Thus it is sometimes difficult to determine which '-ism' a political adherent is 'coming from'. But it is important that we try to make such determinations. When, in particular, we hear talk about the weaknesses or 'defects' of democracy, we have to understand and interpret these allegations in the light of natural biases produced by these polar tendencies. For example, the 'moral mediocrity' and conformism which today's aristocratic-republican discerns in the masses in our democracy, becomes, in the eyes of the 'pure democrat', civic virtue and social sensitivity to the needs, desires and common interests of others; what the aristocrat-republican decries as a consistently low level of decision-making and voting among 'hoi polloi', is, from the very different viewpoint of the pure democrat, the morally and aesthetically satisfying spectacle of people of all dispositions and capabilities participating in government, all in their own way; while aristocrat–republicans warn us about the propensity of citizens to elect officials reflecting and even institutionalising their own weaknesses and vices, the pure democrats view exactly the same phenomenon dispassionately as a great strength of democracies – that rulers are no longer looked upon as charismatic or divine, but as fallible human beings whom we can poke fun at and criticise and even discharge from office; the crass 'materialism' of citizens, which the nobler natures look upon as the result of shallowness and bad breeding, becomes for our egalitarian–democrat the natural and assiduous effort to make material sufficiency – which in past ages has been the *sine qua non* for aristocratic mores, culture and morals – common property for all; and the unusual frequency of changes in policy, the multiplicity of compromises produced by changes in public opinion, which appear to the aristocrat to smack of fickleness and/or lack of principle, are seen by the democrat as the unparalleled ability of a real democracy to keep in touch with what is really going on, and make swift and appropriate adaptations, or even tactical retreats, where these are called for. On the other hand, when the 'pure democrat' in our government protests impersonal and aloof administrative power-politics or lobbying by the wealthy or 'conflicts of interest' in the upper echelons of government, the 'aristocrat republican' will be able to metamorphise all such 'apparent defects' into indisputable virtues in the light of reflections on the need for specialisation, expertise, personal interest, initiative, resourcefulness and/or the effective manipulation of power in government.

There are, of course, certain developments possible in a 'mixed' government such as our own, which would swing the balance so preponderantly to one side that a 'mixture' would scarcely remain. Thus, for example, although a certain amount of political apathy in our citizenry could spell 'natural lack of interest among the masses' for the aristocrat–republican, and 'freedom to participate at one's own discretion' to the pure democrat, there will be some point in the growth of 'intensity of apathy' beyond which all institutional bipolar relativism disappears and the government becomes a 'democracy' or a 'mixed democracy' only in name. If, for instance, the fairly widespread apathy of 'the American people' in national elections were to continue to increase, eventually 'democracy' in the sense in which we have ordinarily been using the term would no longer exist on the national level, and indeed would no longer be an appropriate and effective government for *such* people; an enlightened aristocracy or relative anarchy would no doubt be the 'best' form of government relative to the needs and desires of the people.[12] Conversely, as we already indicated in Chapter 7, if there were some 'totalitarian' system of government characterised by widespread and informed citizen participation, and if we could *determine* that this actually was the case, we would have to conclude that *this* government was 'totalitarian' only in name, i.e. that it was democratic behind a facade of totalitarianism; and those of us who look upon democracy as the 'best form of government' would have to award the laurels of excellence to the totalitarians.

Hopefully, as some futurists and evolutionists conjecture, evolution itself may produce some higher form of government, surpassing democracy as we know it now. In the meantime, the most prudent, the 'best', course to follow is a judicious neo-Solomonian balancing of the prime polarities that seem to become manifest eventually and inevitably, openly or latently, in government.

A polarity is not a mere antithesis. In physics and electromagnetism, polarisation is associated with the release of energy potential, and the motion or actualisation that follows from this release. In human affairs, there seem to be certain natural and constructive types of opposition or polarity (social 'polarisation' unfortunately often has a negative connotation) which can engender optimum balance and actualisation in societies. Hegel's much-misunderstood *Philosophy of Right*, still stereotyped as merely a handbook for Prussian authoritarianism, is a good example of an attempt to understand the modern state in terms of an essential 'dialectical' polarity – the constructive opposition between the individual and subjective, on the one hand, and the objectivity of socio-political institutions and establishments, on the other. But Hegel did not have a democratic model in mind.

In the more specific analysis of the dynamics or dialectics of democracy attempted in this book, we have pointed to, and concentrated on, one particular polarity as primordial and pivotal – the polarity between:

(1) *Populism and élitism*, with its many and varied exemplifications or synonyms (egalitarianism and libertarianism, direct and representative democracy, majoritarianism and minoritarianism, democracy and republicanism). Advocates of one or the other '-ism' typically work in an either/or framework for the furtherance of their own nostrums. The conservatives of the US, for example,would consider it beneficial for democratic society if the programmes of liberals were jettisoned to allow maximum freedom for the sovereign individual, and the liberals would not be too unhappy if they could once and for all overcome the obstructionism of conservatives to inaugurate or implement progressive legislation. But the political philosopher, and perhaps also the astute politician, can and should work within an admittedly more complex and sometimes unwieldly both/and framework, and should be concerned with maintaining and fostering the polarity without undue polarisation. This same observation applies to some of the other corollary polarities we have discussed:

(2) *Bigness and smallness*: while political philosophers from J. J. Rousseau to E. F. Schumacher warn us of the dangers of bigness and impersonal centralisation, philosophers like James Madison and G. W. F. Hegel warn us of the dangers of petty provincialism and blatantly extoll largeness itself as an inducement to cosmopolitanism, civic virtue, and national unity. But the process of expansion carried to an

extreme would lead to machine-like bureaucracy, and the processes of decentralisation carried to an extreme could end in Balkanized conflict or anarchy. The two processes must be mutually coordinated.

(3) *Liberty and equality*: as has been argued above, neither liberty nor equality should be considered in abstraction from property. In the administration of property to promote *both* liberty and equality, we must avoid the oversimplifications of the big spenders who hope to achieve a maximally just society just by shunting the right amount of money to the right places at the right time; as well as the oversimplifications of the free enterprisers who take it as an article of faith that the capital gains of corporations and combines will somehow 'trickle down' to all classes in society. To avoid these oversimplifications we need both the constant prodding of conservatives to trim or cut budgets and the constant efforts of liberals to create, with public funds when necessary, the social and environmental conditions most conducive to maximum equality. As has also been indicated, 'fraternity' might function as a synthesising concept facilitating the coordination of liberty and equality; but the problem of maintaining fraternity in modern megapoli and super-states is colossal. The odds at present do not seem to favour Marshall McLuhan's prediction that the new electronic media would eventually condition a world-wide 'global village' mentality, which might hopefully facilitate fraternity on the larger scale.

(4) *Religion and secular life*: I am using the term 'religion' in a wide sense here, to refer to (a) habits of meditation and reflectiveness geared to staking out for the indivdual an *inner sanctum* which is impervious to external encroachments, and (b) types of associations geared to fostering an individual and communal perfection which transcends that obtainable in ordinary civic life. Admittedly, religion in the sense I have just adumbrated could refer to other than organised religions; but the important thing is that this definition could not refer to the state-as-religion or to the liaison of the individual with his state. For a great democratic 'contribution' of religion is the fact that it helps to guarantee that there will always be an individual, private sphere, ruled by ideals and goals transcending those of the state; that adherence to the state will be spontaneous and discriminating; that the secular will be freed from trying to ape the prerogatives of God (universal providence, omniscience, omnipotence, impeccability, etc.); and that there will be constant communal bulwarks against the sometimes attractive possibility of simply identifying one's own personal interests with those of one's state.

(5) *Libertarian democracy and social democracy*: the democratic devotion to freedom and self-determination can have ironical results. It is not inconceivable that a consistent libertarian may find himself in a position where he has to support a socialist, even a communist, government, provided it is broadly-based and participatory. Not to do so would be to betray his own criterion for justifying governments (namely, the selection and control of the governments by the people). Not to do so would also be to send a message to communists and socialists that the Allendes and Dubčeks will not last long, and hence only the ruthless among them, who care nothing for democratic processes, will be able to survive.

* * *

If these polarities are factual and ineluctable, it would seem that the best form of government would be one that recognised and felicitously fostered and balanced the polarities themselves, especially the first and pivotal polarity. Governments other than democracies have done this occasionally. History provides us examples of monarchies and aristocracies which combined competent and trained rule with sensitivity to the wishes of the general populace. But the great contribution of democracy, as it has evolved, has been (a) removing royal birth or titles and, to some extent wealth, as the final 'test' for competence and expertise; and (b) developing more systematic means for assuring popular consent and participation than were available under even the most paternal and sensitive monarchies or aristocracies. At present, the tests which 'Western' democracy has developed for leadership (possession of constitutional qualifications, law-abiding citizenship, and especially popularity) and the channels it has developed for popular participation in government (constitutional and legal guarantees of rights, voting, referenda, the power of initiative and recall) appear to be preferable to those found under Marxist socialism (although it should be kept in mind that the latter has also done away with privileges based on birth and wealth, and far from being indifferent to popular consent, has even gone to extremes in orchestrating such consent). But 'Western' democracy is imperfect also. In particular, more systematic tests for the competence and responsiveness of leaders and representatives could be developed, and more reliable channels for determining the wishes of the people regarding policies, laws, and issues (not just regarding the politicians who will lead) is necessary. And all the democracies and 'democracies' of the world must deal with two pressing international problems: (a) the fact that no leadership, no matter how competent or expert, can now deal with the complexities of nuclear warfare (the initiation and execution of which has largely been entrusted to computers), and (b) the fact that no reliable channels exist for investigating the possibility of an international consensus on some international issues – a consensus which, if it is not, *should* be of interest to all national leaders who characterise themselves as democratic.

One important second-order polarity, concerned with the interpretation of the five polarities just considered, should also be mentioned, and will serve to conclude our analyses.

(6) *The 'adversary interpretation' and the 'consensual interpretation' of polarities*: (a) It is possible to view the above polarities as necessary evils, as ineluctable antitheses, fully in keeping with the nature of democracy as a massive organised adversary relationship – as has been suggested e.g. by Schumpeter. And (b) it is also possible to view the same polarities as regrettable, eventually surmountable contradictions, diagnosed and criticised by philosophers such as Rousseau and Marx, who idealise democracy as a massive consensual relationship, or extension of human communitarianism.

It is conceivable that one or the other of these polar interpretations may win out. But it is also conceivable that the very polarisation between these two *interpretations* may also be maintained in a state of homeostasis or constructive opposition, engendering and perpetuating vitality in theorising about contemporary democratic societies,[13] just as a democratic society itself may demonstrate its vitality by artfully fostering a constructive opposition, within its partisan groupings, of the more essential, constituent polarities which they manifest.

NOTES

1. There is some unavoidable ambiguity involved in the use of the term, 'relative', with respect to government, as T. L. Thorson shows in *The Logic of Democracy* (NY: Holt, Rinehart & Winston, 1967) ch. III. For instance, we could contend that democracy makes the individual absolute, while totalitarianism makes him relative. But when reference is made in common parlance to an 'absolutist' form of government, authoritarianism or autocracy is usually implied; while democracy is often designated a 'relativistic' form of government. Democracy is *essentially* relativistic, in the sense that it makes government relative to the desires of the people.

However, as W. J. Stankiewicz points out in *Aspects of Political Theory* (London: Macmillan, 1976, pp. 17ff), one can also say that democracy makes the *vox populi* 'absolute'. A similar play on words is evident in Anthony Quinton's distinction (in 'Disputation on the Future of Democracy', *Great Ideas Today*, *The Encyclopaedia Brittanica*, 1978, p. 57) between 'relative' democracy (democracy in which there are proper counterbalances to majority will) and 'absolute' democracy (pure majoritarianism which, e.g. in contemporary England, would lead to oppression of blacks). A Leninist might conversely contrast the 'absolute' democracy to be attained in the final classless stages of communism, with the 'relative' democracy attainable now under the Soviet 'dictatorship of the proletariat'. But both Quinton and our hypothetical Leninist, in referring to their candidate for the 'absolutely best' form of government, would mean by this phrase a government which would be best for the people even though coming into conflict with the presently emerging actual desires, needs, etc., of the people concerned.

2. William Earnest Hocking uses the term, 'relative', in a parallel fashion, but emphasises the fact that ideas of the state as 'absolute' result from subjective intuitions of present potentialities in a state, while 'relativistic' approaches to the state result from the necessity for compromise among those who have different perceptions of what the state should be. See Thigpen, *Liberty and Community*, ch. 1. Mortimer Adler in 'A Disputation on the Future of Democracy' (*The Great Ideas Today*, 1978) p. 27, tries to overcome this standard dichotomy between 'absolute' and 'relative' by developing the paradox that the state through education and social legislation should bring the less-than-ideal citizens up to the ideal level, so that 'the best form of government absolutely is also the best relatively for every human group'. But he relativises his own insight by also observing (ibid., p. 24), 'either a child has enough intelligence for liberal education through the Bachelor of Arts degree, or he does not have enough intelligence for democratic citizenship'.
3. F. Patrick Hubbard, 'Justice, Limits to Growth, and an Equilibrium State', in *Philosophy and Public Affairs*, Summer 1978.
4. 'The Justification of Democracy', from the *Monist*, LV, 1 Jan. 1971, p. 21.
5. See *Democracy*, ch. 1.
6. See Roberto Mangabeira Ungar, *Knowledge and Politics* (NY: Free Press, 1975) Part I.
7. Yves Simon, *Community of the Free*, W. Task tr. (NY: Holt, 1947) p. 149.
8. This position is reflected throughout Dye and Ziegler's *The Irony of Democracy*, and Dahl's *Preface to Democratic Theory*.
9. See e.g. ten Hoor's *Freedom Limited*, p. 47, and Carl J. Friedrich's *Man and his Government*, p. 342. Friedrich warns that too much emphasis on the side of order in a society will eventually and paradoxically result in disorder, or chaotic change which takes the society unawares.
10. The terms 'democratic' and 'republican' as applied to the two polar trends, are being used not necessarily as a designation of twentieth-century party affiliation or sympathies, but as an indication of a general politico-social gravitation towards (a) maximal grass-roots participation

in government, or (b) more specialised élite control over government, respectively.

11. Perhaps it would be useful at this point to recall the distinction made by John Dewey between the 'old liberal' (the *rough* equivalent of today's 'libertarian') and the 'new liberal' (one who recommends highly structured and organised, or even – like Dewey – socialistic measures for achieving political equality). The fact that 'liberal' has come to mean something so completely different than it originally meant may be taken as further evidence of the enduring conflict of élitism and populism within liberalism, as well as in other 'isms'. John Dewey, who was never able to reconcile his socialistic political tendencies with e.g. his educational philosophy which emphasised extreme decentralisation and individualism, is a perfect example of the ambivalence of the 'new liberal'. See Alfonso Damico, *Individuality and Community: The Social and Political Thought of John Dewey* (Gainesville: University of Flordia Press, 1978) chs 5, 7. But if Everett Ladd and Charles Hadley are correct, the 'new liberalism' has also undergone an evolution, so that now we must distinguish between the old new-liberalism (i.e. New Deal liberalism) and the new new-liberalism (oriented to traditional egalitarian values, but less nationalistic, less bureaucratic than previously). See *Transformations of the American Party System* (New York: Norton, 1975). Roland Pennock (*Democratic Political Theory*, p. 510n.) sees this final version of liberalism as actually a throwback to the liberalism of J. S. Mill, but refuses to use the term 'liberal' because of the ambiguities involved. Pennock's refusal can perhaps be best understood if one considers the fact that Ronald Dworkin in his book on political–legal theory (*Taking Rights Seriously*, 1977) uses the term 'liberal' throughout the book in the old sense (i.e. as synonymous with what is often called 'libertarian' now). Perhaps there is something to be said for using terms in their chief contemporary, rather than their original, meanings.
12. If Rousseau is correct (*The Social Contract*, III, 3), a government would have to be in the hands of 50–100% of the people to qualify technically as a 'democracy'. Thus if national election in a country brought out typically only 30–40% of the eligible voters, one could argue that, names aside, the government would be technically an aristocracy or oligarchy.
13. Jane Mansbridge's *Beyond Adversary Democracy* (NY: Basic Books, 1980) theorises from this latter standpoint and actually tries to work out the possibilities of homeostasis through illustrative case-studies.

Bibliography

M. Adler, A. Quinton and M. Cranston, 'A Disputation on Democracy', *The Great Ideas Today* (Encyclopaedia Britannica, 1978).

Allen, Glen, 'Beyond the Voter's Paradox', *Ethics*, LXXXVIII, October 1977.

Aptheker, Herbert, *The Nature of Democracy, Freedom and Revolution* (NY: International, 1969; London: Central Books, 1968).

Ardrey, Robert, *The Social Contract* (NY: Atheneum, 1970).

Arendt, Hannah, *On Revolution* (NY: Viking, 1965; Middlesex: Penguin, 1973).

Bercovitch, Sacvan, *The Puritan Origins of the American Self* (New Haven and London: Yale University Press, 1975).

Bethel, Tom, 'Burning Darwin to Save Marx', *Harpers*, December 1978.

Bloch, Ernst, *Atheism in Christianity*, Swann tr. (NY: Herder & Herder, 1972).

Boorstin, Daniel, *The Genius of American Politics* (Chicago and London: University of Chicago, 1953).

Brecht, Arnold, *Political Theory: the Foundations of 20th Century Political Thought* (Princeton University Press, 1959).

Brittain, John, *Inheritance and Inequality of Material Wealth* (Washington, DC: The Brookings Institution, 1979).

Brown, Norman O., *Love's Body* (NY: Vintage, 1966).

Burham, Walter, 'Thoughts on the "Governability Crisis" in the West', *The Washington Review of Strategic and International Studies*, July 1978.

Ceaser, James W., 'Political Parties and Presidential Ambition', *The Journal of Politics*, August 1978.

Charlesworth, J. (ed.), *The Limits of Behaviorism in Political Science* (Philadelphia: American Academy of Political and Social Science, 1962).

Cline, Ray S., 'A New Grand Strategy for the United States', *Comparative Strategy*, I, 1 and 2, 1978.

Cohen, Carl, *Democracy* (Athens: University of Georgia Press, 1971).

Cranston, Maurice, 'Political Philosophy in Our Time', *The Great Ideas Today*, Hutchins and Adler, eds (Chicago: Encyclopaedia Brittanica, 1975).

Dahl, Robert, *A Preface to Democratic Theory* (Chicago and London: University of Chicago Press, 1956).

Damico, Alfonso, *Individuality and Community: The Social and Political Thought of John Dewey* (Gainesville: University of Florida Press, 1978).

Djilas, Milovan, *The New Class* (NY: Praeger, 1957).

Dworkin, Ronald, *Taking Rights Seriously* (Cambridge, Mass.: Harvard University Press; London: Duckworth, 1977).
Dye, Thomas and Ziegler, H., *The Irony of Democracy* (NY: Wadsworth, 1970).
Frankel, Milton, *The Democratic Prospect* (NY: Harper, 1964).
Friedman, Milton, *Capitalism and Freedom* (Chicago and London: University of Chicago Press, 1962).
Friedrich, Carl J., *Transcendent Justice: the Religious Dimension of Constitutionalism* (North Carolina: Duke University Press, 1964).
Friedrich, Carl J., *Man and His Government* (NY: McGraw-Hill, 1963).
Galbraith, J. K., *The New Industrial State* (NY: Signet and Middlesex: Penguin, 1968).
Garrett, Roland, 'Anarchism or Political Democracy: the Case of William Goodwin', *Social Theory and Practice*, I, Spring 1971.
Gay, Peter, *The Dilemma of Democratic Socialism* (NY: Collier, 1970).
Goodwin, Richard, *The American Condition* (NY: Doubleday, 1974).
Hamilton, A., James Madison and John Jay, *The Federalist Papers* (NY: Anchor, 1961).
Harrington, Michael, *Socialism* (NY: Bantam, 1973).
Hegel, G. W. F., *Philosophy of History*, Sibree tr. (NY: Dover, 1956).
Hoffmann, Stanley, *Primacy of World Order: American Foreign Policy Since the Cold War* (NY and Maidenhead: McGraw-Hill, 1978).
Hubbard, F. Patrick, 'Justice, Limits to Growth, and an Equilibrium State', *Philosophy and Public Affairs*, Summer 1978.
Hutchins, R. M., Adler, M. J. and Bird, O., 'The Idea of Equality', *The Great Ideas Today* (Chicago: Encyclopaedia Britannica, 1968).
Ingersoll, David E., *Communism, Fascism, and Democracy* (Columbus, Ohio: Charles Merill Publishing Co., 1971).
Kainz, H., *Ethica Dialectica* (The Hague: Nijhoff, 1979).
Kainz, H., *The Philosophy of Man: a New Introduction to Some Perennial Issues* (Tuscaloosa: University of Alabama Press, 1980).
Keech, W., *Winner Take All: Report of the Twentieth Century Fund Task Force on Reform of the Presidential Election Process* (NY: Holmes & Meier, 1979).
Kristol, Irving, *Two Cheers for Capitalism* (NY: Basic Books, 1977).
Koch, Adrienne, *The Philosophy of Thomas Jefferson* (Chicago: Quadrangle, 1964).
Kornhauser, W., 'The Politics of Confrontation', in *The New American Revolution* (NY: Free Press, 1971).
Lakoff, Sanford A., *Equality in Political Philosophy* (Mass.: Harvard University Press, 1964).
Lively, Jack, *Democracy* (NY: Capricorn, 1977; Oxford: Blackwell, 1979).
Locke, John, *Second Treatise on Government* (Indianapolis: Bobbs-Merrill, 1952).
Macpherson, C. B., *The Life and Times of Federal Democracy* (Oxford University Press, 1977).
Macpherson, C. B., *The Real World of Democracy* (Oxford University Press, 1972 and 1975).
Mansbridge, J., 'Democracy among Friends', *The Center Magazine* (The Center for Democratic Institutions; January/February, 1979).

Margolis, Michael, *Viable Democracy* (NY and Middlesex: Penguin, 1979).
Megill, Kenneth A., *The New Democratic Theory* (NY: Free Press, 1970).
Michener, James, *Presidential Lottery* (NY: Random House, 1969; London: Secker & Warburg, 1970).
Mill, John Stuart, *Considerations on Representative Government* (Indianapolis: Bobbs-Merrill, 1958).
Mill, John Stuart, *On Liberty* (Indianapolis: Bobbs-Merrill, 1956).
Monist, the, LV, January 1971, general topic: 'Foundations of Democracy'.
Morgenthau, Hans, *The Decline of Democratic Politics* (University of Chicago Press, 1962).
Morgenthau, Hans, *Dilemmas of Politics* (University of Chicago Press, 1970).
Morris, Charles, *The Pragmatic Movement in American Philosophy* (NY: Braziller, 1970).
Mortimore, G. W., 'An Ideal of Equality', *Mind*, LXXVII, 1968.
Myers, Henry A., *Are Men Equal?* (Ithaca, NY: Cornell University Press, Great Seal Books, 1963).
Norton, Thomas James, *The Constitution of the United States: its Sources and Application* (NY: Committee for Constitutional Government, 1965).
Nozick, Robert, *Anarchy, State and Utopia* (NY: Basic Books, 1974; Oxford: Blackwell, 1982).
Oakeshott, Michael, 'The Masses in Representative Democracy', in *Freedom and Serfdom*, A. Hunold (ed.), R. Stevens tr. (Dordrecht, Netherlands: P. Reidel, 1961).
Peirce, Neal T., *The People's President* (NY: Simon & Schuster, 1968; London: Yale University Press, 1981).
Pennock, J. Roland, *Democratic Political Theory* (Princeton University Press, 1979).
Pickles, Dorothy, *Democracy* (Baltimore: Penguin, 1972).
Plamenatz, John, 'Some American Images of Democracy', *The Great Ideas Today 1968* (Chicago: Encyclopaedia Britannica, 1969).
Plamenatz, John, 'The Uses of Political Theory', in A. Quinton's *Political Philosophy* (Oxford University Press, 1967).
Publius II (Justice Owen J. Roberts, John F. Schmidt, and Clarence K. Street), *The New Federalist* (NY: Harper & Row, 1950).
Quinton, Anthony, ed., *Political Philosophy* (Oxford University Press, 1967).
Rawls, John, *A Theory of Justice* (Cambridge, Mass.: Harvard University Press, 1971; Oxford University Press, 1973).
Riemer, Neal, *A Revival of Democratic Theory* (NY: Appleton-Century-Crofts, 1962).
Rossiter, Clinton, *Alexander Hamilton and the Constitution* (NY: Harcourt, Brace & World, 1975).
Rousseau, *On the Origin of Inequality* (First Part).
Rousseau, J. Jacques, *The Social Contract* (Harmondsworth: Penguin, 1969).
Schurmann, Franz, *The New American Revolution* (NY: Free Press, 1971).
Schumpeter, Joseph, *Capitalism, Socialism and Democracy* (NY: Harper, 1950; London: Allen & Unwin, 1977).
Schumpeter, Joseph, *Politics and Markets: the World's Political Economic Systems* (NY: Basic Books, 1977).

Selucký, Radoslav, *Marxism, Socialism, Freedom: Towards a General Democratic Theory of Labour-Managed Systems* (London: Macmillan, 1979).
Sherover, Charles, *The Development of the Democratic Idea* (NY: Mentor, 1974).
Simon, Yves, *Community of the Free*, W. Trask tr. (NY: Holt, 1947).
Stevenson, Charles, *Ethics and Language* (New Haven: Yale University Press, 1944).
ten Hoor, Marten, *Freedom Limited* (University of Alabama Press, 1954).
Thigpen, Robt., *Liberty and Community* (The Hague: Nijhoff, 1972).
Thorson, Thomas Landon, *The Logic of Democracy* (NY: Holt, Rinehart & Winston, 1967).
Tocqueville, Alexis de, *Democracy in America* (NY: Mentor, 1956).
Toynbee, Arnold, *Experiences* (Oxford University Press, 1969).
Tufte, Edward, *Political Control of the Economy* (Princeton University Press, 1978).
Ulam, Adam, 'U.S.–Soviet Relations: Unhappy Coexistence', in *Foreign Affairs*, vol. 57, no. 3, 1979.
Ungar, Roberto Mangabeira, *Knowledge and Politics* (NY: Free Press, 1975; Middlesex: Collier-Macmillan, 1977).
White, Morton, *The Philosophy of the American Revolution* (NY and Oxford: Oxford University Press, 1978).
Wills, Gary, *The Inventing of America* (NY: Doubleday, 1978 and London: Athlone Press, 1980).
Wittfogel, Karl August, *Oriental Despotism: a Comparative Study of Total Power* (New Haven and London: Yale University Press, 1957).
Wokler, Robert, 'Perfectible Apes in Decadent Cultures: Rousseau's Anthropology Revisited', *Daedalus*, vol. 107, no. 3, Summer, 1978.
Wolff, Robert Paul, *In Defense of Anarchism* (NY: Harper Torchbooks, 1970).
Wollheim, Richard, 'Democracy', *Journal of the History of Ideas*, XIX, 1958.

Subject Index

Author Index

www.ingramcontent.com/pod-product-compliance
Lightning Source LLC
Chambersburg PA
CBHW020434290526
45785CB00002B/851

* 9 7 8 1 4 5 0 2 7 6 4 0 5 *